ALSO BY SPRINGS TOLEDO

The Gods of War

IN THE CHEAP SEATS

FEBRUARY 4   **TUESDAY**   **PRICE 2d.**

BIG FIGHT CROWD: CALL FOR POLICE

From the personal collection of Tommy Burns,
former welterweight champion of Australia.

IN THE CHEAP SEATS

Boxing Essays by

Springs Toledo

Foreword by Jim Lampley

Published by Tora Book Publishing
ISBN 978-0-9543924-6-8

Cover Design by Lloyd Lelina of Pixelwurx Graphic Design © 2016

Cover photograph: Match of boxing. France, 1937-1938 (photographer Gaston Paris, Getty Images)

For Mom

Contents

Foreword
by Jim Lampley

Of all the uncomfortable evidences of fallout from the artistic disappointment that was Floyd Mayweather versus Manny Pacquiao, one of the most unsettling was an article by accomplished boxing journalist Richard Hoffer published twelve days later. The headline asserted, "Mayweather v Pacquiao shows that boxing writing is on the ropes."

You can begin a response to that with the obvious reality that in the age of cyber language and the one-hundred-forty-character attention span, all writing is, to some degree or another, on the ropes. But in the vast preponderance of the verbal expression world, there is a great deal less at stake than in the corner to which Hoffer refers. Boxing is different.

Most sports reporting, like basic news reporting, is more a recitation of facts and figures than an expression of the inner reaches of conscious and unconscious thought. For ninety-five years, gloved prizefighting evolved as an attraction devoid of the numerical profiles so prevalent and productive in the marketing of other sports. We knew in the 1970s exactly how many yards O.J. Simpson was gaining, how many points Bill Walton was scoring, and how many batters were striking out in the face of Nolan Ryan. But until the mid-1980s, no one was even attempting to tell us how many jabs Sugar Ray Leonard threw in a round or how many power punches Muhammad Ali absorbed from Joe Frazier. Boxing writers, more than other sports reporters, painted word pictures to replace for their readers what numbers told them about other sports. The attraction of that for wordsmiths was magnetic.

It's redundant now to enumerate all the illustrious writers who have striven to express the compelling drama of the prizefight. It suffices to say they were all drawn by the fundamental simplicity of the competition. Two men (or women) are going to face off half-naked under hot lights and attempt to communicate to each other their courage, their capability to inflict and withstand pain, and their level of irrational self-belief. The forum within which they do it is something that at times mimics ballet, at other times Greco-Roman wrestling. But in its capacity to reveal the character of the combatants, with heads uncovered and the evidence of traded punches gradually and increasingly visible on their faces, boxing is unique. Great writers seek metaphors which illuminate the human condition to readers sophisticated enough to grasp them, and few metaphors are as graphically accessible as boxing.

So in lamenting the effects of modern transmission and deteriorating standards of expression on boxing writing, Richard Hoffer is not, in general, off base. But to suggest great boxing literature no longer exists is a fallacy in the same league with the popular mantra of general sports commentators who are fond of repeating that "boxing is dead." As a global enterprise, boxing is arguably more alive than ever, but that doesn't matter to observers focused mostly on their own markets. As a vehicle of inspiration for writers, boxing is more varied than ever because of the spectacular breadth of locations and life experiences from which the fighters now emerge.

Would A.J. Liebling and W.C. Heinz have found inspiration in the colorful arcs of Third World superstars like Manny Pacquiao and Román "Chocolatito" González? Would Red Smith and Damon Runyon have seen societal significance in the American emergence of post-Soviet stars Gennady Golovkin, Sergey Kovalev, and Vasyl Lomachenko? Would Ernest Hemingway and George Plimpton have shown readers how to identify with the quest for prominence of post-Mayweather talents Terence Crawford and Deontay Wilder? How about Brooklyn's Danny Jacobs and his feat of beating both cancer and Peter Quillin back-to-back? Of course they would. These stories are in every way as communicative and instructive as those of Benny Leonard or Rocky Marciano. They just exist in a different narrative envelope, for an audience more constantly bombarded and distracted by countless forms of competing messages, an audience less appreciative of artistry than of immediacy.

Boxing does have numbers now, provided since the 1980s by CompuBox. And to the degree that those numbers become a crutch for writers whose editors don't want them to paint pictures with words, yes, that has happened. But that in no way establishes that the flame of ring poetry has flickered and died. And without diminishing the credits and reputations of as many as a couple of dozen ringside scribes whom I would deem still capable of evoking deep thought and real emotion with their reporting on fights and fighters, I will boil down the response to Hoffer's doomsday premise to a singular observation: maybe Richard Hoffer hasn't read Springs Toledo.

There are quite a number of literate boxing observers who have spent years in the gym, hitting people and getting hit. There is no shortage of boxing writers who have immersed themselves in classic literature and studied to learn the historical precepts and fundamentals of storytelling craft. There are plenty of ring devotees who have gone back and read their predecessors, from Virgil to Mark Kram, and have filtered their poetic emotions into an analytical view of the unique experience of fighting. Almost all of them have read Liebling and Heinz. Some, like Springs, have painstakingly done all these things, to put themselves into the most credible possible position from which to speak to human hearts about courage and triumph, frustration and pain. You can't do more to prepare yourself to write boxing than Springs Toledo has done.

The results are here in these pages. In them you will encounter provocative assertions and editorial choices, and because boxing doesn't exist without the acceptance of risk, with some of them you will internally disagree. That is a natural, inevitable product of Springs's fearless strong-mindedness, and it is part of what makes his work worth reading. Elsewhere you are sure to find observations and premises that are as thunderously on target as a Jack Dempsey left hook. That is part of why you will reread some entries and share them with others who appreciate ring lit.

The proud tradition of building stories on the foundational metaphor of the ring has in no way died. It lives on in the words of hardy souls whose attachment to the sweet science is invulnerable to the ridicule of the many who have forgotten boxing's indelible place in the fabric of global civilization. Front and center among them, for my humble money, is Springs Toledo.

IN THE CHEAP SEATS

Introduction

Two researchers at the University of Utah recently took a stand against their peers in academia, against those who shake their fists at all things masculine and keep their heads down on the train to work.

Michael Morgan and David Carrier's "Protective buttressing of the human fist and the evolution of hominin hands" was published in the *Journal of Experimental Biology* in 2013. It challenges the widely accepted theory that our hands evolved to improve manual dexterity and asserts that the size, shape, and dimensions of the fist are well adapted for "competing males to strike with greater force and power while greatly reducing the risk of injury to the hand." The critics came out swinging. If, so to speak, the male fist evolved to throw left hooks to win mates and protect resources, then why aren't masculine faces shaped like catcher's mitts?

Biological Reviews published the answer. "Protective buttressing of the hominin face" begins with Morgan and Carrier knocking down another theory, also widely accepted, that the human facial structure is the result of our ancestors' diet of tough foods such as roots and nuts. The lower jaw muscles, they point out, are actually "overbuilt" for chewing though not for shock absorption —in other words, they help reduce the risk of dislocation when a left hook lands.

What's more, the marked differences between the sexes in those anatomical areas associated with fighting, including not only the hand and jaw but the neck and nose, likewise point toward nature's deference to our age-old inclinations —in other words, the fists and heads of boxing's detractors can be admitted as evidence against them.

If males, rivals all, are hard-wired for aggression and to some degree built for it, then boxing itself further buttresses us against injury. Padded leather gloves protect the bones of the hand and defensive drills make slipping blows second nature, but boxing, as a discipline, also tempers the impetus toward lethal force and deters street confrontations (would you attack someone who can lay you out on the sidewalk?). It has proven to be nothing less than a social good to the disadvantaged; it reroutes delinquent pathways and redirects the urges of young men, particularly those without the guiding hand of a father.

If modern boxing has a father, it is the Marquess of Queensberry John Sholto Douglas. A revolutionary set of rules created under his name in the 1860s would eventually end the brutal era of bare-knuckle marathons in favor of gloved contests and three-minute rounds. He was instrumental in civilizing a baser form of the sport and saw its value in civilizing our baser instincts. "I have no objection to see a good fight with gloves, or without them for the matter of that," he said over the hue and cry of polite society. "Yet England may regret some day that her sons should substitute for the use of their fists the first deadly weapon that comes to their hands."

Theodore Roosevelt understood its value to society just as well, and like Queensberry enjoyed mixing it up himself. He "did a good deal of it" at Harvard, frankly admitting he couldn't compete at the amateur championship level and was a trial horse for those who could. As President, he regularly invited White House aides to go rounds with him and wouldn't officially hang up his gloves until he was fifty. "I regard boxing whether amateur or professional, as a first-class sport," he wrote in 1920. "I do not regard it as brutalizing." Far from it; when he was New York City's Police Commissioner, Roosevelt praised it more than any modern-day social worker has ever praised a state-funded juvenile diversion program. In his experience, "the establishment of a boxing club in a tough neighborhood always tended to do away with knifing and gunfighting among the young fellows who would otherwise have been in murderous gangs."

It is no surprise that Roman Catholic priests and police officers took the lead in introducing boxing to fatherless boys in church basements and Police Athletic Leagues. A cavalcade of the greatest champions we've ever seen owed much to the collar and the badge, to yesterday's social workers who embraced biological facts and traditional ideas about masculinity.

Things have changed. And not necessarily for the better. The church and its patriarchal authority have been under siege for the last half-century. The authoritarianism of too many police officers has diminished their standing in those communities that need them most. One need only sit in on a sociology elective in any university this side of Texas A&M to see masculinity itself on the ropes. Yet boxing continues to be the sport of choice to have-nots around the world. Why? Is it because of some genetic deficiency or intrinsic bloodthirstiness? No, though some anti-boxing arguments floating down from ivory towers are every bit as narrow as the phrenologists' were during Queensberry's era.

The answer is found in poetry, not science.

It's found in boxing's remarkable capacity to touch the observer. Boxing is a powerful analogy for hard realities below the poverty line, where whatever you have today may be gone tomorrow, where violence is more than a statistic, where the commitment to stay in school, resist the lure of gang life, and become a success begins with the willingness and the ability to stand alone.

Pull away from socioeconomic class and see that the iconic figure of the boxer speaks to anyone who struggles; which is to say he speaks to all of us. Prone, he tells us we're not alone. Rising, whether to victory or just to beat the count, he tells us we can too.

It's a matter of perspective really, and it improves the farther back we go. Perhaps that explains why the cheering at a boxing match is loudest where perspective is best —in the cheap seats.

SPRINGS TOLEDO
Boston, 2015

Dempsey through the Ropes, 1923. George Bellows

SOMETHING TO CHEER ABOUT

One-Sided Glove Affairs

Life loves the liver of it.
—Maya Angelou

Providence-based promoter and President of Classic Entertainment & Sports Jimmy Burchfield had a birthday Friday. He took the celebration to the Twin River Event Center in Lincoln, RI where he sponsored a boxing show called "Braggin' Rights" and gave his cake to the patrons: tickets were slashed and included redeemable free play at the casino. Jimmy may have regretted the whole thing as he stood in the ring and was subjected to a rendition of "Happy Birthday" by local boxing notables Joey Spina, Reinaldo Oliveira, Bobby Harris, and Vinnie Paz.

The first bout of the evening featured local cruiserweight Jay Holland (3-0) against a thirty-six-year-old opponent from Youngstown, Ohio. A left hook by Holland told all and sundry that whatever it is in Youngstown that gave us Tommy Bell, Tony Janiro, Ray Mancini, and Kelly Pavlik was not bequeathed to his opponent. The bout was over in fifty-seven seconds.

It looked like the makings of another one-sided affair when Diego Pereira (4-0) landed the kind of left hook to the liver of Ramon Ellis (0-3) that would convince most to quit the ring and apply for community college. Ellis's face contorted and down he went. In a bigger casino in Las Vegas that very evening, Robert Guillen went down after Guillermo Rigondeaux landed the same shot to his liver. Such a shot has ended at least one budding acting career: when aging heavyweight Earnie Shavers was in the ring with Sylvester Stallone auditioning for the role of Clubber Lang in Rocky III, he tapped him on the liver. Stallone left the ring and threw up in the men's room. Shavers was handed a ticket home.

When Ellis went down he assumed the classic posture of submission on one knee while the referee counted. Someone nearby commented "He ain't getting up from that." Usually he'd be correct, though after glancing at the program, I knew he'd be wrong here.

"He'll get up," I said. "He's a Philly fighter."

Guillen is from Arizona; he was counted out. Stallone is an actor; he was crazy to invite Earnie Shavers into the ring in the first place. The Philadelphian not only got up and survived the round, he landed an overhand right that persuaded him, he said afterward, to "lay back and counter." Nevertheless, I counted at least four more shots to the right upper quadrant of Ellis's abdominal cavity, though Ellis later told me he was deflecting them by keeping his right elbow tightly drawn to that side.

Pereira won a unanimous decision after four rounds. Ellis will have to decide whether to risk his health again for the elusive first win. After the bout, I asked him a candid question:

"Why did you get up?"

"I wanted to *win* that fight! I'm *not* an opponent and I *refuse to be* an opponent." (emphasis his)

Ellis's nickname derives from his initials. "RTE" stands for Ramon Thomas Ellis, but he said it is also an acronym for "Really Terrible Ending." On Friday night he didn't fight well enough to win, but he did fight well enough to avoid a horizontal defeat, which would have injected his acronym with irony.

Super middleweight and University of Rhode Island graduate Vladine "Bad Boy" Biosse (2-0) entered the ring as if he were preparing to enter a cannon at the circus; complete with shiny robe, go-go dancing girls, swirling blue lights, and a crowd hoping to gawp at the misfortune of a misplaced net or an involuntary nap. The URI mascot "Rhody the Ram" preceded Biosse down the aisle and hopped about the ring where the 0-2 opponent stood by patiently.

The two-time loser came all the way from South Carolina but looked like an envelope without an address. Two left hooks and a flying mouthpiece later, he found an address on the canvas. Although he got up before the count of ten, his vim and vigor took the full count and the ref waved the fight off. Biosse posed on every turnbuckle and left the ring with nary a bead of sweat on his forehead and the hopping ram in tow.

The co-featured bout was supposed to be a rematch between Mickey Ward's nephew Sean Eklund and the "Puerto Rican Sensation" Eddie Soto (12-0). Eklund got sick, and the ripped-and-ready Soto was matched with a slightly built stand-in named Darrell Martin (4-10).

Martin was willing to engage the Puerto Rican Sensation up to the moment he got dropped with a right hand in the second round. After that he became a poor man's Willie Pep, though he was not unimpressive in evading the lefts, rights, ring posts, and kitchen sink Soto threw his way. However, Martin was all butterfly and no bee. Soto swung, missed, and grew frustrated, but at least he was trying. It soon became clear that Martin wasn't concerned with the prospect of losing so much as he was with making Soto look bad winning. He even made the referee look bad refereeing after three near collisions. In the sixth, Martin stopped floating and started stinging. Soto's eyes lit up when his quarry finally got in range and landed another hard shot that got Martin floating again to a decision loss.

The main event featured junior welterweights "Hammerin' Hank" Lundy (14-0-1) and local favorite Josh "Steamin'" Beeman (4-4-3). At the pre-fight press conference, Beeman was anything but an accommodating host for the Philadelphian, choosing instead to dub himself the defender of the realm of Rhode Island. Lundy, the guest, took offense at such hubris and immediately morphed into a great winged dragon at the podium. The crowd of innocents gasped as he gave his word that he was going to "whoop" the local favorite's gluteus maximus. Then he leaned into the microphone and hissed, "That's all I have to say." The microphone melted. The dragon stalked back to his cave to sharpen his talons.

At fight time, Lundy ran down the aisle into the ring and was pacing about when swirling lights popped on in the back of the event center. The crowd erupted, and the music proclaiming the entrance of Josh Beeman was louder than the crowd. I had vainly hoped for a trumpet blast but was instead subjected to a cacophony of disjointed thumpings set to obnoxious bravado. All heads were turned toward the far end of the aisle, but there was no sign of the defender of the realm. A minute and a half passed and the cheering was dwindling away to nothing when he appeared off to my left. I wondered whether his delay was due to the disarray of his team or his nerves.

Round one saw him crouching behind a palisade of arms while Lundy was shooting out a jab like a forked tongue. Lundy soon found a breach and demonstrated an understanding of siege warfare by undermining the walls before him. The ancients called it sapping. We call it body punching. Beeman wasn't doing much besides slinging a few hooks to force not victory but temporary relief. He seemed relieved to get the first round behind him.

I don't know if he knows boxing history, but if he did he'd have had a deeper concern. Lundy and the imperial beard jutting out from his chin reminded me of Archie Moore —his rising jab, shoulder rolls, cross-armed defense, a concentration on the body, lots of slipping and a stance that saw his right crooked up across his chest.

If Beeman was expecting to begin heroics after shaking loose the first-round jitters, he forgot his sword. Lundy was already in control to the point where he was dropping his hands, squaring off, and hitting Beeman at will. Before the bell for round three, he was dancing in time with the go-go girls stationed at the neutral corners.

Aficionados of the sweet science become familiar over time with the technical goings-on of a bout. The more astute among them eventually develop into uncertified psychologists. They can, for example, tell you the difference between an outclassed fighter and a veteran counterpuncher. Both appear reluctant to engage though for one it's purposeful and for the other it's a reflection not of strategy but of anxiety. The whys and wherefores are quite simple: any time any fighter throws a shot, he leaves a window open. The experienced fighter will make painful deposits through those open windows until the outclassed fighter is dissuaded from mounting an assault of his own. Inclement conditions see him batten down the hatches. For him it's a long fight.

The difference between the outclassed fighter and the veteran counter-puncher comes down to this: if his visage is unmarred, he's probably implementing a grand strategy. If it's lumpy, he's probably outclassed. Beeman's was lumpy.

By round four, Hammerin' Hank was living up to his audacious nickname and throwing five or six rapid-fire combinations to the body and head, spinning off, landing lead uppercuts from the outside, and switching from orthodox to southpaw. In the fifth round, the invader of the realm ended the bout with a left hook to the body and then brought it up to the head. The defender of the realm absorbed both shots, then took a few tottering steps on tottering legs and collapsed in a heap. His face contorted in pain and he clutched his right side. Ten seconds later his tribulation was over, his failure complete.

Lundy was still channeling Archie Moore during his post-fight interview. He's a raconteur. "I'm must-see TV!" he proclaimed. "I'll go into anyone's backyard with my zero and I come out with my zero!" When asked what shot finished Beeman, he said it was the left hook to the body —to the liver. Lundy is officially calling out THE RING's number one rated Timothy Bradley.

Sloan Harrison, out of the Kingsessing Recreation Center in Philadelphia, is Lundy's trainer. "What I love about [Lundy]," Harrison said, "is that he listens in the gym, he's a nice, clean-cut guy, and in the fight he follows instructions." No faint praise from a trainer who has been plying his trade in Philadelphia boxing gyms for over thirty years.

Among his favorite fighters is none other than Archie Moore.

July 18, 2009

Me and Mr. Jones

"….we got a thing goin' on…"

The first time ever I saw Roy Jones Jr. was on a Sunday afternoon twenty years ago. He fought a Mormon journeyman on NBC's Sportsworld and by the second round, curiosity had turned to amazement. By the fourth, I was craned forward on my chair and my decade-long infatuation with his fighting style began. The journeyman tried as valiantly as the next thirty-one men Jones would face, and like every one of those thirty-one, he never had a chance.

The wave of public support Jones was surfing after the 1988 Olympics crested early. He was called "the best kept secret in boxing" but his star was dimming in step with the refusal of his father —also his manager, promoter, and trainer— to allow him to face a fighter who wasn't a has-been, a never-was, or a not-as-advertised. Then in the summer of 1990 Jones made quick work of Derwin Richards, whose record of 18-1 turned out to be as fraudulent as his name. The opponent's name was actually Tony Waddles; his record was actually 0-2.

NBC took note and terminated his contract early. "It got to be a joke," Kevin Monaghan, the network's former boxing director, told Bernard Fernandez. "They were just so incredibly cautious." Roy Jones Sr. proved immune to the criticism. After all, Jones was barely twenty-one years old at the time and the objective was to groom him for greatness, not throw him to the lions. Big Roy pointed to Andrew Maynard, a gold medalist from the 1988 Olympics who turned professional, was managed by Sugar Ray Leonard, and was as hot as Jones. But Maynard was rushed. A few weeks before Jones fought the fraud, Maynard was knocked out and his career never recovered.

Jones's first fight on HBO was his second without his father as manager. In fifteen seconds Jones landed an overhand right that sent Percy Harris down in sections. Harris spent four rounds about as upright as a man atop a raft on a stormy sea. It was over before the fifth. Charley Burley, one of history's great uncrowned champions had died only weeks before at the age of seventy-five, or had he? Jones's feinting, springing, blasting unorthodoxy was so eerily similar to Burley's style I thought voodoo was afoot.

Six months later Jones faced THE RING's sixth-rated contender Bernard Hopkins.

Hopkins was a twenty-eight-year-old middleweight and already a full-blown technician. He was far more aggressive then than now and yet was shy about engaging Jones, realizing perhaps that Jones had a penchant for poleaxing rambunctious opponents. Hopkins made the mistake of standing off and boxing Jones instead of neutralizing his speed with aggression. He may as well have tried to catch a hornet with chopsticks. He lost 116-112. Hopkins would not lose again for a dozen years but this loss had much to do with his obscurity for the next decade. He toiled and boiled in the shadow of his conqueror. The experience wasn't for naught because Hopkins realized then and there that being a technician without a strategy was akin to being an engineer without a blueprint. That realization, conspicuously absent in the Jones fight, is still serving him well in middle age. While Hopkins stewed with secret regret, Jones stayed busy and stepped forward to meet the greatest challenge of his career.

James "Lights Out" Toney was boxing's angriest super middleweight. With his hair-trigger temper and an eating disorder that would eventually see him swell up to Pillsbury proportions as a heavyweight, he was a complicated study. He had a master's degree in the sweet science, with a slipping and sliding style sophisticated enough to check no less than Mike McCallum. Launched into stardom by a left hook that put stars in the eyes of Michael Nunn and took the stars out of the eyes of Nunn's Hollywood backers, Toney was coming off a career-best performance against former light heavyweight champion Prince Charles Williams. None of that mattered. Jones had an easy night. By moving away from Toney's right, leading with left hooks instead of jabs, and destroying his timing, Jones made Toney look like Charlie Brown. The gap on the scorecards was wider than it was in the Hopkins fight.

With this win, Roy Jones Jr. was crowned king of boxing and I won a gentleman's bet.

"...we both know that it's wrong..."

Jones became known as "Reluctant Roy" in the mid-1990s. It wasn't undeserved. Only three years earlier, he was in a rush to make up for lost time spent on set-ups; in 1995 he changed his mind. According to a source whose reliability is a mystery, Jones demanded three million to fight ex-champion Michael Nunn, who was offered a paltry $125,000. Jones, in other words, priced himself out of reach. Meanwhile, super middleweights Nigel Benn, Chris Eubank, Steve Collins, and Frankie Liles were all active circa 1994-1996 and like Jones, they were all rated in the top five by THE RING and had a trick title at one point or another (though it was Liles who emerged as the true champion of the division from August 1994 until June 1999). But it was Jones, the superstar, who was calling the shots. Despite the fact that he was at his peak, he didn't fight them. Not one of them. Armed with an HBO contract that guaranteed millions regardless of who he fought, Jones fought an assortment of secondary contenders and municipal workers.

Liles was trained by Freddie Roach. Steve Collins was too. Roach tried to set up fights with Jones but his calls were not returned. After Collins turned thirty years old, he grew a goatee and became twice the fighter he was, rechristening himself "The Celtic Warrior." Dangerous enough to defeat Eubank and Benn twice by the end of 1996, he had a shillelagh with Jones's name on it. After Jones cruised to a stoppage of a thirty-nine-year-old moonlighting police officer, Collins defiantly climbed into the ring. As Larry Merchant was interviewing Jones, Collins said "I'm here, Roy." Merchant ignored

Collins but apologized to the HBO audience for the sorry fight. "I always thought Jones was chinny," Collins told *Boxing Monthly*. "From the way he fought, Jones himself knew if he got caught flush, he'd go, and shied away from certain scenarios in the ring."

Some critics will tell you that Jones had already revealed a pattern of avoidance, that the early termination of his contract with NBC was merely the opening act to a career where maximum gain would be sought for minimum risk. They overlook the fact that Jones heard this criticism before, fired his father, and soon afterwards faced down two all-time greats in Hopkins and Toney. Yet the question remains, why didn't Jones face the iron at super middleweight after 1994?

The answer is found in the aftermath of the tragic Nigel Benn-Gerald McClellan fight early in 1995. McClellan was knocked out in the tenth round and slipped into a coma. He emerged from it blind, almost completely deaf, brain damaged, and in a wheel-chair. Jones and McClellan were amateur rivals (McClellan holds a Golden Gloves victory over Jones) and Jones shared a bond with him that only ring rivals can understand. He will not visit McClellan until he retires, though he has donated generously to the McClellan trust fund. Jones was haunted by what happened for years. He be-came less willing to hurt anyone and less willing to get hurt himself. "I don't need to [visit Gerald]. It would make me quit boxing," he once said. Glory began to taste too much like blood so he began to distract himself with safer pursuits like rap music and basketball. "If I fought like I was looking for a place in history," he said in an interview with *Esquire* in 2003, "it would ruin me as a person."

His fabled entry into the light heavyweight division only added to what was becoming the fable of his all-time greatness. His first challenger was Mike McCallum who was three weeks shy of his fortieth birthday. His next bout was against Montell Griffin. Ed-die Futch, the ten-to-one underdog's chief second, had done his homework, probably in the same yellowing notebook where he de-constructed the undefeated Ali on behalf of Joe Frazier and the undefeated Evander Holyfield on behalf of Riddick Bowe. Like

Steve Collins, Futch saw clues to Jones's psychology in his style that suggested an unusual fear of getting hit, so he instructed Griffin to feint and bull him. Jones was not comfortable, ended up losing by disqualification, and old Eddie Futch ruined another perfect record. Boxing aficionados still talk about the body shot that caved in Virgil Hill's ribs. What is less remembered is the fact that Jones refused to fight Hill as late as 1996. Hill lost his light heavyweight throne to the undefeated Dariusz Michalczewski in 1997 and suddenly Jones signed —to fight the loser. Michalczewski was the true light heavyweight champion from the moment his hand was raised in victory over Hill, but instead of fighting him, Jones was chasing trick titles.

He was still chasing trick titles when he challenged heavyweight John Ruiz. Ruiz made good use of his thirty pound weight advantage by charging Jones in the first round. A shootout at the end of that round saw the heavyweight clinching Jones after the smaller man landed the bigger shots. He charged less in the next three rounds, and after a flush right made his knees knock, Ruiz, like Hopkins and Toney, fought Jones as if Jones were King Kong.

Antonio Tarver was no Fay Wray. When Tarver became the number one rated light heavyweight contender in a WBS organization, Jones's manager Murad Muhammad wrote a letter questioning Tarver's credentials to be number one. Read between the lines. Jones didn't want to face Tarver and wouldn't for three years. There is a pattern here that raises an eyebrow. Jones allegedly priced himself out of a Michael Nunn fight. He didn't fight top super middleweight contender Frankie Liles though he held close wins over him in the amateurs. Then he tried to block Tarver, a fellow Floridian, from stepping into his ring. Now ask yourself what these three had in common: all three were tall southpaws with skill.

The first bout with Tarver was competitive, and I saw no controversy in Jones's win. Tarver did. During the pre-fight instructions of the rematch, Tarver lobbed an unforgettable verbal shot across the bow: "I got a question —you got any excuses tonight, Roy?" The lanky southpaw would leave room for none after a left hand rendered Jones semiconscious and the fight was stopped in the second round. Mortality beckoned in his next fight. Glen Johnson barreled straight at Jones, not unlike Collins would have, never allowing the stylist to dictate the pace. In the ninth round, the horizontal ex-hero looked like he was dead.

By then, my fascination with Roy Jones Jr. had ended. Nine long years passed before he added the victory over John Ruiz to his victory over James Toney, and those weren't enough to justify the dim-bulb comparisons between Jones and Sugar Ray Robinson tossed around in certain quarters. Ruiz, I believed at the time, was just a plumper cherry picked from a tree in the meadow of Jones's casual career and when finally tested by two skilled and gritty fighters, Jones was ruthlessly exposed.

He's about to be exposed again. Due in part to the choices he made over his long career and also to the confused medley of faux championships that sports writers inexplicably prop up, Jones never took a true divisional throne. He never defeated the rightful champion at middleweight, super middleweight, light heavyweight, or heavyweight and he never fought the next-best contender when he was rated first or second by THE RING in any of those divisions. What he has is a collection of belts that are beside the point. No boxing historian with a dime's worth of sense can deny it. I know I can't.

This realization, which came on the heels of his two knockout losses, forces a question. Is Jones an all-time great fighter? I thought so; maybe I still do. But he was no Superman. We both know that's wrong.

"…but it's much too strong to let it go now…"

Jones didn't want to be wrong. And his decision to fight Antonio Tarver a third time proved it. Most civilians get bitten by a dog once and then get jittery around a Pekinese. Not Jones. He was knocked out twice and returned seeking to avenge one of them at thirty-six years old. That's courage. Old embers from my long-gone teenage years began to glow.

His comeback is more impressive when you look more closely.

Roy was never a technician despite the common error of many analysts who claim otherwise. Jones was, however, among the greatest pure athletes to ever grace the ring. He had timing, rhythm, flash, and demon speed backed up by shocking power. His leaping left hook needed no microphone to pick up the THWAP. But there's a cost to such gifts. Athletes like Jones typically have shorter primes than technicians for the simple reason that technicians are less dependent on the powers of youth. Amazingly, Jones hasn't even made any notable adjustments to his style. He's a step or three slower but still showboating, still shooting from the hip, and yet had enough left to drop Joe Calzaghe in the first round. And he made me doubt my own judgment that he fears punchers when he thoroughly tamed Jeff Lacy with his hands down.

Next up is Danny "The Green Machine" Green, a cruiserweight. Jones has an illuminating message for Green: "I've got some thing to prove." Indeed. Old Jones is raging against the dying of the light. He is on redemption's path, rebuking those who accused him of avoiding dangerous fighters during his prime, and perhaps, just perhaps, performing private penance for doing exactly that.

As the conclusion of his career draws near, I'll be watching —an old fan, a new fan, a critic with bated breath.

> *We gotta be extra careful*
> *that we don't build our hopes up too high*
> *because he's got his own obligations*
> *and so, and so, do I*
> *...Me and Mr. Jones.*

August 31, 2009

A Ghost in the Machine

Blue-collar hero Kelly Pavlik prefers the hard way. He takes the stairs. Over the past few years he has trudged up the most perilous stairwell in sports like a laborer burdened with blunt instruments. He doesn't complain. He sees what there is to do and he does it with an uncomplicated resolve common in places like Youngstown, Ohio.

Youngstown. Back in 1922, "Pavlik" was one of two hundred seventy-six Slovak surnames on mailboxes in the Lansingville section of the city. Their descendant remains close to home despite the fame and fortune his fists brought over the past few years. He stays while others leave. In 1930 the steel industry was strong and the population peaked at one-hundred seventy thousand. It has declined sixty-seven percent since then. Thirty-three years ago its economy collapsed when too many businesses moved away seeking cheaper labor, when it stubbornly stuck with what it knew even while empty shells of furnaces and foundries began dotting the landscape. At this writing, almost one in four of its inhabitants is scrounging below the poverty line because the city failed to keep up with changing times. Youngstown didn't diversify.

During training, Pavlik leaves his parents' house to do early morning roadwork, a skeletal figure in a hoodie running past the haunted old mills.

Pavlik didn't diversify either. He didn't need to. He climbed out of the basement where so many nameless fighters toil in dim lights and defeated first a contender and then a champion. Hometown support helped; those blunt instruments dangling at the end of his arms helped more.

The contender was Edison Miranda, a puncher known to absorb and deliver punishment in equal parts. The champion was Jermain Taylor and thousands of Pavlik's neighbors left Youngstown for Atlantic City to see Pavlik's coronation. It was a fight for the ages. Five rounds after teetering on the brink of a knockout loss, Pavlik hit Taylor with an assembly line of punches that dropped him like a crane would scrap metal.

That was 2007. The first white middleweight king since 1980 threw a belt over his shoulder and thanked the city he loves. "I still get goose bumps thinking about the fans who came out," he said.

The excitement a white working-class American champion stirs up in the boxing world is something to behold. More complex in its origins than racism and less noble than patriotism, it was confirmed when Pavlik handled Taylor again in the rematch. Still, purists of every pigment remained suspicious about the new king's aptitude. The former king's style was never sophisticated. He never learned his craft well enough to become a technician or a stylist, and instead relies on natural ability. His legs, for example, move as if he is playing tennis. He is not malicious and the nom de guerre of "Bad Intentions" doesn't make him so. He is spirited but never mean, competitive but never do-or-die. Pavlik's search-and-destroy robotics were beyond him.

Nothing is beyond the master craftsman who stood atop the next flight on Pavlik's perilous climb. Bernard Hopkins, then forty-three, met him at super middleweight. With tools as sharp as Pavlik's are blunt, Hopkins used a multifaceted approach to deal with a straight-thinking, straight-punching method, and spun him as easily as a hustler spins a hick. Afterwards the master craftsman pushed his glove into Pavlik's chest. "You are a great middleweight champion," he said. "Keep your head up and keep fighting."

Pavlik did his best. He made two low-risk defenses and stopped both but couldn't dispel the disillusionment that had set in among fans. The word was out, even in Youngstown. "Heavy-handed Pavlik is one-dimensional," it said. "He has trouble with skilled boxers."

Argentinean Sergio Martinez is a skilled boxer. He is also a former professional athlete who evolved into a stylist on wheels with a rhythm all his own and a soccer player's sense of placement. Those wheels and that placement were more than enough to make the feared and avoided Paul Williams look like, well, Kelly Pavlik.

The wrench that Hopkins so casually tossed into Pavlik's machine had to be removed and Pavlik would try to do it the hard way, by prevailing over a fighter who promised to be even more wrenching than Hopkins. It was a callused hand that signed to fight Martinez.

By the end of the ninth round, he looked as if the Ohio state bird had crashed headlong into his face. "I couldn't see," he said in the minutes after his crown was surrendered to Martinez, as blood was wiped off his face.

Youngstown had Black Monday; Pavlik, Bloody Saturday. A local historian might suggest to us that he made the same mistake his city made decades ago when it stuck with what it knew in an expanding market and ended up losing what it had.

Now twenty-eight years old, Pavlik has gone as far as he can go with what he has. He'll have to reconfigure his equipment to meet styles more sophisticated than simple punchers and over-eager athletes because the word is out. Geometry and mobility can break him down. If nothing changes, he himself will end up a scuffed stair for the newly ascending.

He must diversify.

Youngstown, like its favorite son, has been struggling in a ruthlessly progressive world that left it brooding by broken windows. This year newspapers are reporting that hope is rising for the city; new initiatives are developing technology-based companies with some success. Kelly Pavlik wants to become a part of the renewal plan.

There is hope for him. Boxing's landscape, littered though it is with dented husks, has a history animated by willing spirits and resurrections.

April 19, 2010

The Boxing Marvel
Speaks to Maravilla

I have always found that no opponent is very dangerous if you can keep a left hand sticking in his face, get in and get out, and prevent him from getting set for a punch.
—Jack Britton, 1923

History is as circular as a boxing ring is square. Imagine a master boxer known for his matinee-idol appearance, great legs, and a crowd-pleasing willingness to mix it up. Legions of Spanish-speaking fans north and south of the border would picture "Maravilla," Sergio Gabriel Martinez. However, the English translation of "Maravilla" is "the Marvel" and the description could just as well conjure up memories of the "Boxing Marvel" Jack Britton. Britton, any boxing historian can tell you, fought at least three hundred forty-four times between 1904 and 1930 and was welterweight champion of the world.

The thirty-five-year-old Martinez is a former welterweight champion of Argentina scheduled to face Paul "The Punisher" Williams in New Jersey on November 20 in a contest the odds makers call even money.

Ninety years ago Britton was also thirty-five and fighting in New Jersey.

Familiar Spirit

Celebrated by Jim Jab of the *Pittsburgh Press* as the "master mechanic of mittdom" and the "monarch of maul," Britton faced a man who "towered over him in everything but boxing skill." Despite his age, Britton still managed to "outfeint, outfoot, and outwit" his opponent. "The crowd that jammed the big Jersey armory," the *Associated Press* reported,

> . . . *saw Britton give a masterly exhibition of the manly art. Fast with both hands and feet, Jack outfought Mike [O'Dowd] in all but the third and the seventh rounds. Both at the long range and the infighting, the middleweight found the welterweight too much for him. Even when Britton threw boxing to the winds and stood toe to toe with O'Dowd and swapped wallops, Jack seldom came out second best.*

Britton's winging hooks staggered his opponent and the rare rounds he lost seemed to be times he was resting. When his opponent crowded him Britton would dazzle the crowd with the skills that earned him his nickname. He'd pick his shots and counter inside; he'd lie back patiently and then explode with combinations to the body and head. Frustrated, his opponent would punch more and connect less while Britton evaded the shots with such mastery that the crowd would break into spontaneous applause. A writer for the *New York Times* thought that O'Dowd's frantic punch rate was carrying the fight until his eyes refocused on Britton, who casually "sidestepped, backed away, ducked and dodged the shower of blows."

No accomplishment in his long career gave Britton more pride than his ability to handle Mike O'Dowd four out of five times. Like Paul Williams today, O'Dowd was routinely avoided back then, but Britton figured that "anyone fast enough to keep him on the move could beat him."

It was his legs. He was known for his legs, even at thirty-five. His trainer, Dai Dollings, was a New York City transplant who had previously trained marathon runners in Wales.

Sergio Martinez is a former professional soccer player and cyclist and he too is known for his legs, even at thirty-five.

Britton proved to be a brilliant student of styles. And well he should have; his trainer taught the great Ray Arcel how to deconstruct boxers and exploit their every move. "Dollings was a smart trainer," Arcel recalled. "He was a fella who'd study the styles of the different boxers. And of course when I started with him, that was the one thing he inspired me with —everyone's style is different, so you must understand the different styles of your opponents. And we used to make a great study, watching these fellas work."

Britton's boxing brain saw him defeat a who's who of great fighters and suffer only one knockout when he was still a teenager. It paid off in other ways too. He became as good, said the *Providence News* in 1923, as Gentleman Jim Corbett was bad at predicting fights. Britton not only anticipated outcomes, he explained why with an expert's eye. When world featherweight champion Johnny Kilbane met the French contender Eugene Criqui, Britton stood alone and predicted an upset by knockout. The chuckles in the press section were silenced at one minute and fifty-four seconds of the sixth round. World heavyweight champion Jack Dempsey was still considered a man-killer that year, and it was a sure thing that he would knock out light heavyweight Tommy Gibbons. Britton predicted that Gibbons's chin would hold up and see him last the distance but lose a decision. He was right. Criqui made his first defense against Johnny Dundee a few weeks after that. Britton said that Dundee didn't have the punch to stop Criqui but that he would win by decision. He was right again.

Britton would have much to say to his modern mirror-image about how to defeat a bigger, younger, and constantly-punching opponent.

Martinez gives up four inches in height and six inches in reach to Williams, whose shots fly in from the third row like dishes thrown by poltergeists and whose stamina pushes the outer limits of human performance. But old-school trainers look askew at Williams's chin. "You know them fighters with long necks and them long, pointy chins," Charlie Goldman once quipped. "They cost you more for smelling salts than they do for food." Williams has been a rebuke to that stereotype. The durability of his chin is both surprising for the observer and demoralizing for the opponent, at least for now.

By all accounts this fighter presents a tortuous set of problems for any fighter today...or yesterday.

What Would Jack Say?

Britton, with an Irish twinkle in his eye, would assert that Williams may have taken a decision against Martinez once but he won't get lucky twice. Luck bows before perfect strategy.

Williams has *tendencies*. He has bad habits. For a man who was able to find the flaws of no less than Benny Leonard, solving Williams's style would be easy. Despite an average punch rate of a hundred per round, Williams is prone to become casual about it. He gets a bit detached as if on automatic pilot. The shots come from all angles, but they can be lazy and wide. Many offensive machines in history short-changed their defense and Williams is no exception. His judgment of distance is off. When he steps inside he drops his guard; and on the outside, where his long body should dominate, he overreaches. Williams's pressure has made him both formidable and feared but it comes with a cost. Pressure fighters are usually designed like badgers, short and strong. They try to compensate for physical disadvantages by fighting at close range where their concentrated strength and stunted reach become advantages. They are not often built like a Great Blue Heron. Williams is. Neither is designed to withstand head trauma.

Britton would politely remind us that Martinez's style is much like his —it is much like an all-time great fighter's. Watching the first round of their first bout is an eerie confirmation of exactly that. Martinez slides in and out to land shots on Williams and then disappears out of range. He steps off at angles and forces the taller man to turn and reset. He drops his arms to his sides. This is vintage Britton.

Britton would also remind Martinez that the last southpaw stylist who faced Williams a second time was demolished in one round.

That version should be anticipated on November 20 —the Avenging Williams. Williams will be as determined and as focused as a heron on a shrimp in shallow water. If Williams is smart, he will spear his man with shots from the shore where he can reach Martinez and Martinez can't reach him. He will try to stun him and if he does, he will wade in behind well-aimed combinations to swallow him whole. Martinez is going to have to be very careful for the first few rounds. Britton had a secret to beating his era's Paul Williams: "He used to murder jabbers," he recalled about O'Dowd, "so when I got in the ring with him I just kept going into him all the time, toe to toe, swinging with his swings and he never got started."

Ted "Kid" Lewis was Britton's arch-nemesis. Twenty-two times they clashed in what became boxing's version of the Hatfields and McCoys. It was Britton who got the better of it, though handling Lewis's relentlessness required wisdom. "I would go one round and box him, the next time I would slug him," Britton said. "I'd slow him up and in the next round switch and speed all over him. He didn't know where he was."

Like Britton, Martinez formulates strategy with his seconds at training camp. He knows the danger of lingering at mid-range because that is where Williams's punches can shock him. (Martinez went down in the first round and got nailed twice at the end of the fourth while lingering at mid-range.) As he tired his legs got flat and that's when victory got away from him. He must fight Williams at opposite distances: outside of the perimeter (that is, outside of that wingspan), ready to connect when the overreaching Williams leaves his head hanging out like a nosy neighbor, and in close around the taller man's chest where he can get rough safely.

Jack Britton's secret strategies defeated two of his roughest rivals; one widely avoided and physically overwhelming, the other an all-action fellow great. He shared those secrets in this séance. Is Martinez listening?

This much is certain: Maravilla and his legs will have to be near

perfect to triumph. If the ghost of the Boxing Marvel is in his corner, they will be.

November 17, 2010

SHAZAM!

"And there was boxing," wrote Louis Golding in 1940. "Thank the Lord, despite the thousand barriers, there was boxing. For I have been a boxing fan just as much as I have been a ballet fan and for similar reasons."

Golding, a British novelist and essayist, was yet another writer who found inspiration in the sweet science. Famous in his day if largely forgotten in ours, he attended the fights when he had nothing to celebrate as much as when he did. What he found there was something inspirational "—and beautiful too," he said, "not less than painting or dancing or drama." Other sports fall short in terms of human performance, whereas "the training that boxing involves," he said, "makes the male body as perfect as it knows how to be." Fighters stand under the lights like "Greek athletes molded in bronze" for tense moments. "And then —and then, their great moment comes," Golding beamed. "Then the moment snaps," and they move.

The moment snapped Saturday night.

When it did, two athletes at the top of their game moved toward ring center. Sergio "Maravilla" Martinez quick-stepped forward and made a halfhearted attempt to touch gloves. Paul Williams galloped in and made a wholehearted attempt to land a right hook. Tall and lean and mean, Williams sought to establish mastery by resolutely refusing to concede space. Martinez and a pair of perfect legs created space. He stepped backward and circled with grace and rhythm.

"It is," said Golding, "in the nature of their movement that one will often find, in first-rate boxing the quality of ballet almost as vigorously controlled within the framework of its own patterns." Replace HBO commentators with classical music and Martinez-Williams II becomes rather like a *pas de deux*. One pursues, the other is coy. The controlled aggression of Williams complements Martinez's dazzling virtuosos. The virtuoso disrupts the movement by sliding back and then in at angles, accompanied by hooks that cut the air and passados thrusting high and low. At times he slips a glove around Williams's waist and they embrace. The punches of both are executed in textbook fashion. Errant blows demonstrate that this is not choreography, though even those are not wanting for elegance.

Maravilla's performance was an inspired one. The ghost of the "Boxing Marvel" Jack Britton seemed to be with him; and a curious artifact that turned up during a post-fight interview confirms that notion. It was a notebook. The Martinez camp kept it out of the hands of inquiring reporters but said its pages contain handwritten strategies to defeat Williams.

I was squinting to get a good look at it, half expecting to see it yellowed with age, half expecting to see Britton's name on it. After all, Martinez operated precisely the way Britton said he should. He had to be a study in contrasts to deal with the all-action opponent. And he was: Martinez fought at opposite distances, outside of Williams's wingspan and inside of it, at his chest. He looped punches over Williams's arms and threw short straight ones in close. He retreated loosely and attacked with gritted teeth. He led; and he countered when Williams led.

Williams fought as expected. And that was his mistake.

He never gave a second thought to anything besides imposing his will. "I felt good," he said afterwards, "and was gonna make it a tough fight." He wouldn't change a thing. "I wasn't gonna try to box him or nothing," he said. "If we fight him again, I'd do it the same way." Manny Steward believed that Williams was fighting a perfect fight. Manny Steward, and this is rare, was wrong. A boxer's style should complement not only his disposition but his physicality. Williams is junkyard dog tough with a motivation beyond the kind typically found in other athletes. The desire to excel is too sterile a description for what he feels; and what he feels was on full display after Martinez landed hard shots throughout their first bout and continued to land them in round one of the rematch. Williams retaliated instantly, unthinkingly. He either has blind faith in his chin or he didn't give a whit about getting hit. His come-forward, defense-be-damned, high-volume style reflects his motivation and his motivation is wrath.

The insistence on trench warfare may match his disposition, but it is an affront to his physicality. Tall and gangly boxers should operate behind their reach because by maintaining distance between themselves and their shorter opponents, they stay relatively safe. That style complements their physical advantages. With proper punching mechanics, it enhances them. Punches cracking like whips at range are perhaps the most lethal that a boxer can develop, and fighters built like Great Blue Herons deliver them best of all. Williams has been shunning what he has and what he is because anger distorts better judgment. He is pretending that he can defy nature with his present style and his trainers have been complicit. He has been a good fighter with great luck.

Great luck bowed to perfect strategy.

Martinez saw that Williams tends to drop his right hand. He tested that theory early by sliding to his right as Williams advanced, then tossing over a left. It landed well enough for him to make a mental note that confirmed his written notes. Williams continued to commit errors common to offensive machines by single-mindedly marching into the danger zone without his guard up. Meanwhile, Martinez locked in his plan and diverted attention away from it by sliding in the opposite direction and varying his shots.

At 2:02 of the second round, the middleweight champion of the world executed his plan. Captain Marvel, cape and all, seemed to join the Boxing Marvel to lend Maravilla a bolt to match his brains.

Williams misjudged his distance, dropped his right, threw a left, and his royal aspirations ended that second. Martinez had skipped rightward to leverage and launch an overhand left, simultaneously turning his head to ride the incoming left, just in case. And then, SHAZAM! Williams collapsed face first on the canvas.

It was déjà vu.

In 1919, Britton scored the only knockout in his series with Ted "Kid" Lewis. It foreshadowed Martinez's exclamatory feat. The relentless Lewis, like Williams, was known for his ability to take a punch. No one expected a stylist to knock him down, never mind out. "Britton," said the *Youngstown Daily Vindicator*, "edged in close and ripped rights and lefts to the body." He "measured his distance accurately, and a long right swing caught the Englishman flush on the jaw." That right was a mirror image of what Martinez threw Saturday night. It was a picture-perfect punch.

After the smoke cleared, Ted "Kid" Lewis and Paul Williams lay on their respective faces, separated from their senses and by nine decades. Deafening crowds stood and lauded the artistry of two boxing marvels.

Sergio Martinez was overjoyed. A crown glimmered atop his head as he was hoisted up onto a second's shoulders shouting "Argentina! Argentina!"

Jack Britton was more restrained. He hurried over to where the referee stood swinging an arm over his collapsed rival, and mimed the count.

November 22, 2010

Something to Cheer About

Erik "El Terrible" Morales hasn't earned significant laurels since he handed Manny Pacquiao his first (and last) defeat on American shores. That was in 2005. Two years later he heard bells in his head after dropping a decision to lightweight David Diaz and promptly retired.

For two and a half years he brooded, stuffed his face, and brooded some more. Then he drank *Tecate* and brooded again. His lean frame pushed outwards and reportedly tipped the scales at two hundred pounds. His pride, bobbing for air in a sea of frothy calories and depression, did not drown. Eventually it burned again.

It was only his shadow that took three victories over nondescript opponents last year. And it was, if you asked any number of boxing writers, foolish pride that prompted him to accept a fight against the very dangerous Marcos Maidana. Maidana, twenty-seven, is a natural light welterweight. The aging Morales is a natural featherweight. With reflexes slowed, timing off, balance tenuous, what was Morales asking for in his decision to fight a relentless man considerably bigger and stronger than anyone he had ever faced before? Had this great fighter's destructive impulses reversed direction?

Before the main event Saturday night, Morales shadowboxed in the dressing room. He was bone dry. His arms were no more impressive than an accountant's and his torso had the consistency of a week-old party balloon. In another dressing room Maidana was a study in strength and virility with tattoos splashed all over his musculature like graffiti on a train. One of them was a gun.

Some said that the ultimate responsibility for Morales's impending doom was our own. What were we asking for when we financed this event, this slaughter? The Morales delusion was unnerving.

Round one hadn't even ended before Maidana landed a hook inside Morales's high guard, causing his right eye to begin closing immediately and just like that the disadvantages of age and size were compounded by the nightmare of compromised vision. By the end of the third, his eye was sealed shut and he had to fight the next nine rounds half blind like Harry Greb, though even Greb had it better than Morales —his handicap was a closely guarded secret while millions saw the condition of Morales's eye in blazing color. His attempts to hide it behind a raised glove were futile; the hard-punching mauler aimed at the tender flesh of the injury and blackened it until it looked like a rotten plum.

In the fifth round, his one good eye boiled with something like rage and a reanimated right fist came hurling out of the past. It struck willful youth, disciplining it, and completely changed the narrative of the fight. And with that, the Morales delusion became something else, something grand, something to stand up and cheer about.

Last February, Morales was asked how he beat Pacquiao. He replied that it was due to "something you don't see often —técnica." *Technique*. "What's important is technique," Morales said. "A lot of Mexicans don't look that good physically, but . . . we know how to fight. It's all about technique. Without a doubt that's the single most important thing for me, technique." It should be the most important thing for every fighter. There is a nuts and bolts way to deal with any style and technicians carry a tool box. During the preliminaries, Nobuhiro Ishida opened his and quickly exposed the limitations of the puncher James Kirkland, giving Japan something to cheer about. Robert Guerrero's wife is cancer-free, and so, with tragedy averted he overcame the swarming style of Michael Katsidis with surgical precision. Despite the riveting violence of an event billed as "Action Heroes," boxing was whispering that it is, always was, and ever shall be a thinking man's sport.

When Morales began lifting up Maidana's head with uppercuts to get it in the range of the right cross, wise novices took notes. They watched him jabbing with the authority of a man accustomed to getting his own way, and throwing the "ole one-two" even if it was only a little faster than their grandfathers' mimicry. Straight punches traveled inside eager arcs to prove again and again the supremacy of technical warfare. In the sixth round, Morales countered and then spun Maidana into a left hook that wobbled him. The crowd roared. I dropped my drink. At the bell ending round eight, the younger, stronger man wandered around the ring in a daze looking for his corner.

Something was happening on the other side of the spectacle. Morales was challenging something beyond flesh, blood, and bone. He was challenging fate. Just before round eleven began, his corner, as surprised as everyone else at Morales's performance but correctly sensing that he was behind in points, prodded him for more. "Even the referee is against you," they said. They told him he needed to knock Maidana out to defeat him. They may as well have told him to tilt the earth. He didn't. He couldn't.

"All of us who watched him know now that man cannot beat down Fate, no matter how much his will may flame," wrote Heywood Broun about another underdog in another time, "but he can rock it back upon its heels when he puts all his heart and shoulders into a blow." Morales was good enough to rock Fate several times on Saturday night. It was thrilling to see. To those who could get on the other side of the violence, it was beautiful to see.

Once again, boxing drew back a bloody veil to reveal hardship and glory sharing the same stage. And we cheered and dropped our drinks because in changing the narrative of this fight, the aging Mexican suggested that we can change our own narratives —our own ultimately dismal expectations— as we contend half blind against mauling life and marching time. He consoled us.

He consoled us even in losing. Fate laughs and tells us that his defeat was inevitable, that *our* defeat is inevitable.

But what matters, damn it all, is not that he lost —it's that he *almost won.*

April 12, 2011

The Most Dangerous Game

By stopping Juan Manuel Lopez in a sequel to their first thriller in April 2011, Orlando Salido gave México yet another victory over national nemesis Puerto Rico. He did it in San Juan while ten thousand Puerto Rican fans surrounded his wife and three judges were set to rob him of a decision. He did it after unhinging Lopez from his senses in the eighth round.

Somewhere up there, Jack Dempsey dropped a harp and burst into applause. Dempsey correctly believed that punchers are made, not born. His theories were published way back in 1950 in a book that explained just how it was that he demolished forty-one men and toppled a giant off the heavyweight throne. No mention was made of iron bolts or plaster of Paris and none was necessary; Dempsey's secrets were of the scientific, not the criminal, type. Many of them were written in longhand on three hundred eighty-four pages when he was a half-starved journeyman staying nights in fleabag hotels. With *Championship Boxing: Explosive Punching and Aggressive Defense*, Dempsey proved that he was serious about self-improvement long before he began attending tea parties with Hollywood softies.

Real power, the kind that dents chins and topples giants, is a product of "fast-moving body weight," said Dempsey; gravity not only gives motion to weight by causing it to fall, it increases its force. He came up with something called the "falling step" where a boxer becomes a puncher by using forward motion and gravity to increase the force of a blow in much the same way that small objects become lethal when dropped from a building.

Salido put these theories into practice Saturday night. I know not whether Dempsey's book was translated into Spanish and found its way into his training camp, but I know what I see and I saw Dempsey's theories in action.

"The hook is the perfect whirling punch," said Dempsey. "It's pure." He distinguished shovel hooks (where the elbow is held tight to the body to shoot upwards in close) from the usual outside hooks. Salido did both. In fact, his left shovel hook was a potent counter to Lopez's jab while his outside hooks came from not only the left, but the right, which is unusual for an orthodox fighter. In fact, three right hooks were landed one after another in the second round and the last one was enough to convince Lopez to back off.

Dempsey backed off from Sam Langford. Like Dempsey, Langford had his own theories of pugilism though his were of the down-home variety. How to win? "Whatever that other man want to do, don't let him do it." So, even as Salido used physics to increase the force of his body-head combinations, he confused "that other man" with strange sights like counter-uppercuts and right hooks.

Lopez wasn't doing much of anything because his head was ringing. Had he recognized his true enemies through the fog, he might have cursed Dempsey and Langford. Instead he placed his faith in a more recent ring general and mirrored his style. But Floyd Mayweather Jr. couldn't help him. Mayweather weathers storms and looks for counter shots, but it's hard to weather a storm that whirls in from both sides and throws unexpected shots; and it's hard to counter a man whose torso is a helical spring. What's more, Lopez insulted Mayweather by being offensive instead of defensive when his back was on the ropes, and so demonstrated the vanity of students who try to amend tried-and-true theories of their betters.

Then came that check hook in the fifth round that dropped Salido and almost made a jerk out of Dempsey.

There was irony in it. Lopez landed it only because he momentarily forgot himself and began to think strategically, like a Hollywood dandy working the floor. Instead of meeting the rushing Salido punch-for-punch, he stepped back and off the perimeter. As Salido's slashing hooks whizzed by, he countered with straight lines and moved. It was a short right that caught Salido blind; and things were suddenly looking up, Salido included.

Fellow Puerto Rican Felix Trinidad watched what had happened from ringside and tried in vain to explain it to those around him. Finally, he began tapping the left side of his chin. (It takes patience to explain to Boricuas how a man moving backwards can accomplish anything at all.)

In rounds six and seven, Salido was whirling again and Lopez was forced to the ropes. Mayweather's dirty tricks, an elbow to the face and a forearm on the back of the neck, proved useless. Lopez was scurrying backwards with a glove pressing down on Salido's on-rushing head but could hold him off no more than a pedestrian can hold off a pit bull. By round eight, Salido was feeling safe enough to get conventional. He began fighting the southpaw like the textbooks say he should, with lead rights.

One minute was left in the round when his punches unhinged Lopez.

Round nine, they say, is a candidate for "Round of the Year." That may be so, but Lopez won't be talking much about it to his grandchildren because he won't remember it. He wasn't there; he was floating above the ring on Cloud Nine watching his automatic arms repeat combinations drilled into him at the Caguas Gym. While Salido was purposefully falling into his punches, Lopez was falling onto Salido and punching with no purpose whatsoever.

The one-minute rest at the end of the ninth was not enough for Lopez to become whole again. It was just enough for his head, jarred again in the opening seconds of the tenth, to send a message to his legs. The message said "collapse, because this guy's pride is gonna kill us both." But pride isn't easily swallowed anywhere in Latin America where the only anatomy that matters in the end looks like two boxing gloves. That's why Lopez got up.

Referee Roberto Ramirez Sr. had to distinguish between that pride and the very real prospect of a ring tragedy. He had a momentous decision to make and only seconds to make it. Luckily, he understood his responsibilities. He deftly continued the standing-eight count even while sidestepping the stumbling Lopez. He turned a deaf ear to the roaring thousands in the Coliseum and looked into the glazed eyes of a defeated fighter.

Then he stopped the fight.

Somewhere up there, Jack Dempsey dropped his harp and burst into applause again. Like Ramirez, the retired Dempsey was the third man in the ring for over two hundred fifty professional bouts. Like Ramirez, he was accused of having an inappropriate gambling interest in the outcome of one of them. And despite his affinity for aggression, he didn't flinch when he stopped forty-eight contests that had become one-sided beatings. Dempsey knew what Ramirez knows. He knew that no one enters the ring without first suppressing the instinct of self-preservation and that some go too far. The referee is there to protect boxers from their own spirits and remind us that boxing is still a sport.

Had Ramirez not understood his responsibilities on Saturday night, Salido-Lopez II would have degenerated into an attrition fight —the kind that ends on a stretcher. Roy Gillespie, Jimmy Doyle, Jackie Darthard, Sam Baroudi, Jody White, Duk Koo Kim, and Francisco "Paco" Rodriguez are only a few of the hundreds with spirits that soared so high they went up through the rafters, leaving loved ones behind to pick up the pieces.

The good sense of Ramirez would have saved many of them.

You can bet on that.

March 12, 2012

Bruce Lee in Boxing Trunks

G*ame of Death*, Bruce Lee's unfinished masterwork, gave us the enduring image of the first international Asian superstar in a yellow tracksuit, ascending levels of a pagoda where assorted challengers await him. On the third level was Filipino-American Dan Inosanto, a friend and student of Lee's who took the role as a favor. The challenger that loomed on the fifth was billed as "The Unknown" and played by Los Angeles Laker Kareem Abdul-Jabbar. Lee's climactic match against the seven-feet-two-inch giant has awed adolescent boys ever since, especially the short ones.

Fans of "The Dragon" didn't miss the tribute last Saturday night. Nonito Donaire made his way to the ring wearing a robe and trunks that recalled Lee's iconic tracksuit. Dan Inosanto, now seventy-five years old, followed close behind while challenger Jeffrey Mathebula—the Abdul-Jabbar of jr. featherweights—loomed up ahead. Donaire admitted to HBO that he'd "never faced a guy who's taller than me, especially not five inches taller than me. I want to figure out that kind of style." He wants to figure out all kinds of styles, "step by step," as if climbing a pagoda.

Donaire, whose abusive classmates in the Philippines and California bullied him into boxing, has become a fighter after Lee's own heart. *Game of Death* was, after all, intended to do more than empower sprouting boys to feel their oats. Lee intended it to showcase a theory of combat that revolves around formlessness, that is, adapting to changing conditions and different styles. "Things live by moving," he said, "and get stronger as they go." Every successive opponent that he conquered in the film symbolically led him to a higher level, a higher state of being. Few got it. He tried explaining his theories on a Canadian talk show in 1971, particularly his desire to teach how to "express one's self honestly, not lying to one's self" but the host was as receptive as a bucket of ice. "This is very un-western," he said.

Nevertheless, Lee's theory of progressive spirituality in the form of combat has been radically applied by another beast from the East. Manny Pacquiao has ascended through boxing's pagoda to seize four true crowns in four weight divisions. Bruce Lee went straight to Pacquiao's head and landed in his hairstyle.

Donaire's receding hairline doesn't allow for that kind of tribute, and he has not, despite the boxing world's penchant for lying to itself, taken a true divisional crown yet. But he too is a disciple. "I want to learn every aspect of who I am and what I can do," he says. He studied film before the Mathebula fight; he studied *Game of Death*. Like Lee against Abdul-Jabbar, he attacked his towering opponent from two ranges, outside Mathebula's reach and pressed up against Mathebula's chest. He angled around, dipped under long hooks, and threw looping shots up where the air is thin to catch that dangling chin.

I was half-expecting him to flick his lip with his thumb.

Boxing was part of Lee's beginnings. He boxed in Hong Kong as a teenager and was good enough to win a tournament involving fifteen high schools in the late 1950s. Inosanto is confident that he could have been a top-ranked lightweight in the 1960s, during the era of Carlos Ortiz. His intensity, speed, and dynamism would have been assets, though what would have set him apart was the "unbelievable power" he could generate despite his size.

In 1959, Lee left Hong Kong and began teaching Wing Chun in the United States. He had not, at the time, evolved out of the traditional school of martial arts with its upright stance and straight-ahead attack and had not yet incorporated the feints, angles, and broken rhythm he would become known for. It took a Golden Gloves boxer named Leo Fong to demonstrate the value of these tactics. He did it by inviting Lee to attack him. Lee rushed forward with chopping hands and Fong simply stepped off to one side and turned over a left hook. It was an epiphany for the young master. Fong would soon convince Lee that the typical martial artist's stance, with the lead hand held high and the back hand held by the solar plexus, was inferior to the American boxer's stance, where the lead hand is low and the back hand is high enough to protect the chin. "I like it because I can't trap your lead hand," Lee told Fong. "Over the next few years," Fong recalled, "Bruce completely changed his primary fighting stance and eventually adopted more of a boxing stance as his own." This happened around the time that Lee began developing his dynamic style.

Boxing –practical, spontaneous, and multidimensional– may have been the impetus that shifted Lee away from traditional forms and toward the fighting system that became Jeet Kune Do.

The Tao of Jeet Kune Do, which is a compilation of his notes, relies heavily on boxing principles. Lee referenced Jack Dempsey and Edwin L. Haislet's *Boxing* (1940) at least twenty times. He reportedly owned more than a hundred boxing books.

He also owned one of the largest collections of fight films in the country and would invite associates to his house for marathon viewings on Wednesdays. "Bruce used to analyze those films," recalled one of them. "We could only take it for a couple of hours, but Bruce could sit there for eight or ten hours and still show the same interest and enthusiasm he showed in the first five minutes." He was capable of mimicking not just the Ali shuffle, but the Sharkey roll, Joe Louis's six-inch punch, and Kid Gavilan's bolo punch (which was, incidentally, another import from the East, as is the bolo itself. Filipino fighters based in California during the 1930s introduced it). Whenever a move interested him, Lee, a southpaw, would rewind the film, stand and turn his back to watch it in a mirror, and practice it. Joe Lewis, a karate champion, attended the "Wednesday Night Fights" hosted by Lee. "Willie Pep, reputed by many to be pound for pound the best boxer of all time," he said, "was the fight-er whose footwork Bruce and I would study."

In round two of Saturday night's bout, Donaire mimicked Lee's dancing footwork. However, Lee's dancing footwork wasn't his own —it was Willie Pep's. Boxing begins and ends the circle.

The sweet science whispered its truths to The Dragon and The Dragon listened. Boxing's impact on Western culture cannot be overestimated. Neither can Bruce Lee's. Lee learned from West-ern culture and then confronted it. "In the United States," he said, "something about the oriental, the true oriental, should be shown." And so it was. Lee singlehandedly redefined the image of the Asian male while the whole world watched and learned. The buck-toothed bowing oddity portrayed on film since Charlie Chan was rolled back in the wake of his fame. It happened as fast as that kick he landed on Kareem Abdul-Jabbar's face. Asian boys suddenly had nothing to be "so sorry" about once he lifted their chins and gave them an image to be proud of; the image of himself, an image they could find in the mirror.

Nonito Donaire was one of them. A bullied child made to feel ashamed of his appearance has evolved into something of an icon himself. He looks in the mirror at Bruce Lee in boxing trunks —and Bruce Lee looks back.

July 10, 2012

The Way of the Jackal

When Nonito Donaire left his corner to face Guillermo "El Chacal" Rigondeaux at the first bell, he took two steps forward and spread his legs. That was the first hint of what he was in for. The Boxing Writers Association of America's 2012 "Fighter of the Year" fought more like John "the Beast" Mugabi than the celebrated boxer-puncher he is. In failing to apply an intelligent strategy or a sustained attack, he was undone. The jr. featherweight throne, which is set above the belts and the nonsense by the *Transnational Boxing Rankings Board* was ripped out from under Donaire by a master counterpuncher.

That wide stance you saw Donaire assume indicated primitive thinking. When Mugabi tried to seize the throne of Marvelous Marvin Hagler back in 1986, Mugabi stood pat as if to say "move me." Hagler, his bald head steaming under Vegas lights, moved him.

Rigondeaux moved.

Standing a little over five feet four inches and sporting a professional record shorter than that (Rigondeaux was 11-0 at fight time), he made the best argument yet for long apprenticeships in the amateur ranks (his record is reportedly 243-4) and is a future addition into the best parade in boxing, a parade led by supreme stylists Joe Gans and Jack Britton, by Willie Pep and Pernell Whitaker, where banners flap in the wind and declare that the alpha asset in the ring is skill; and the more advanced it is, the better.

The Pep/Whitaker fan base is smaller than the bloodthirsty, balcony-busting Tyson/Gatti crowd, but more urbane. Gil Clancy, the late Hall of Fame trainer and expert analyst for both Showtime and HBO was among them. His commentary during the Hagler-Mugabi broadcast can shine a light on Saturday night and reveal just how it was that Rigondeaux defeated Donaire.

"Marvin is moving the way he should, he has to constantly move to his right and use that jab —make Mugabi reach for him."

Hagler's right jab was designed to stunt Mugabi's offense. Rigondeaux's jab was used more as a distraction. He shot it out like he was shadow boxing, at times tapping Donaire's glove like an amateur taps an opponent's headgear for points. Its purpose was to entice a counter from Donaire and counter that counter. In round four, he half-extended his lead hand like an old-school fighter from the 1900s. That was also an enticement.

Rigondeaux, a southpaw like Hagler, did not move to his right as Clancy would have expected. He moved to his left, though with a purpose. He knows to move to his right and has in previous bouts against orthodox fighters, but he made a tactical adjustment against Donaire. Why? Gil Clancy has the answer.

"We always say a left hook is the way to beat a southpaw, and Mugabi's got a vicious left hook."

Donaire's got a vicious left hook. Rigondeaux was aware of the danger enough to break with tradition. More concerned about Donaire's left hook than his right hand, he moved to his left to circle away from it. He didn't do it without thumbing his nose now and then: in the first round he shifted to his left, and as he went, he landed a right hook. Donaire's counter left hook fizzled behind him.

Rigondeaux also changed directions, suddenly and just as easily, to his right. In a laudable demonstration of boxing improv, he slid to his right off a right hook. (It is the same principle a certain writer uses when climbing out of his Camaro. He swings a leg to the pavement, places an elbow at the egress, spins out with a grunt, and hopes no one notices.) When Donaire tried to counter the right hook with a left hook, Rigondeaux would merely dip his head under it while sliding away.

". . . Mugabi is allowing Hagler to move the way he wants to move."

Donaire was allowing Rigondeaux to move the way he wanted to move. He waited like a stationary bike in a bedroom, like a monument to fizzled intentions. What was he waiting for? Donaire, a natural counterpuncher like Rigondeaux, was waiting for a mistake to capitalize on. He got a sum total of one. When Rigondeaux got tangled up with him in the tenth round, he stood square long enough for Donaire to wing a left that knocked him off balance and to the canvas. But then, Michelangelo got paint in his eyes during his own exertions.

Rigondeaux was allowed the freedom to experiment during the bout. In the first round, he fought on a dime at mid-range to find counters and send messages. Those one-twos were warnings about what was coming if Donaire got fresh. By the second round, he had moved outside, just off the perimeter, to set bait with dummy jabs and loose hooks. Donaire was constantly forced to turn and reset. He was mesmerized by mobility and wary with the memory of an overhand left that landed in the first round. His beastly posture remained, even if he was tamed.

"It's the pattern of the fight that counts . . ."

Rigondeaux finished the fight as if he had just finished a brisk walk in Central Park. Except for two significant punches landed by Donaire, both of them unorthodox and therefore not detected by advanced radar, Rigondeaux emerged unscathed. This demands a closer look.

How did a man with a preference for fighting off the back foot tame a beast? Despite his own sense of being wronged by boxing, Rigondeaux does not fight with the righteous rage that motivated Marvin Hagler. Where Hagler was willing, Rigondeaux is not. "He seen me still smiling," Hagler said about a Mugabi blast. "I like that kind of stuff. I love a good fight." Rigondeaux fights like someone suffering from chiraptophobia, and yet managed to convince Donaire that his aggression would be punished.

Rigondeaux's offense was triggered by Donaire feints and posturing as much as by his actual assaults. When Donaire thought he saw a bull's eye, Rigondeaux would read his intentions and respond. In rounds four and six, Donaire mounted an attack and was surprised when Rigondeaux finished the exchanges with an exclamation point. There was something else that surprised Donaire: Rigondeaux's defensive aptitude was actually elevated during heated exchanges. The pattern was almost invariable —under fire, Rigondeaux grits his teeth. He gets low, feints a shot with one hand while moving in to shoot his other hand, and then dips his head as he slides off to a safe angle. Donaire could only miss, absorb a shot flush to the face, and then miss again.

With his left hook neutralized early and his head bouncing backwards from counter shots, Donaire began acting in a way that a behaviorist might call learned helplessness. He seemed to believe the counterpuncher in front of him was doing him a favor by remaining in a defensive posture, by sparing him from Hagler-like ferocity. And in a gesture of appreciation, he ignored his corner's pleas to pressure Rigondeaux. He willingly lost eleven of twelve rounds because the jackal was not worth provoking. The jackal had broken his spirit.

It was an anticlimactic championship bout –the kind that brings groans from the Tyson-Gatti crowd– but it was, said Rigondeaux, an exhibition of skill for "the people who know boxing"; like Gil Clancy.

As for the vanquished, he called the new king's performance "... *beautiful* ..."

April 13, 2013

Stugots

A red tear trickled down Paulie Malignaggi's cheek Saturday night. I saw it in the fourth round as he got up from the first knockdown. The referee was calling out the standing eight, but Paulie ignored him; he was busy making sure his legs still worked.

The welterweight who clubbed him down walked backward to a neutral corner and never took his eyes off Paulie. I never took my eyes off him. He's a juggernaut, short and wide like an image in a funhouse mirror, shoulders like boulders, no neck. He reminded me of someone I got to know recently, someone from the ferocious forties. Shawn Porter was barreling in like a little tiger —like *the* Little Tiger, Aaron Wade. His left hooks and right hand blasts were ruffling old fight reports scattered around my living room floor.

Wade went barreling through three divisions between 1935 and 1947. He began his career as a welterweight and then advanced to middleweight and light heavyweight. Porter has traveled the same path through the traditional weight classes, only in reverse. Their paradigms are also similar. Wade eventually became a Christian minister. Porter held a prayer meeting in his corner after the fight was stopped and was overheard saying, "We pray for Paulie's health in Jesus's name."

Paulie was lying nearby, under the ropes. I thought about Willie Pep. Great though he was, Pep too was laid out after Sandy Saddler got him good. It was October 29, 1948. "I started out feinting as usual to get a feeling for him and he ignored it completely and caught me cold," Pep said. "I was completely surprised. He knocked me down twice before the fourth round and then he stopped me."

Porter and Wade. Paulie and Pep. "The Sweet Science," said A.J. Liebling, "is joined onto the past like a man's arm to his shoulder."

The *science* of the sweet science is also joined onto the past. We learned early that master boxers like Pep toy with plodding punchers, though swarmers and pressure fighters present real problems. They're disruptive. The boxer uses pizazz punctuated by jabs to con his opponent into a pace and rhythm designed to sap his spirit. But disruptive fighters don't buy what's being sold. The swarmer closes in rapidly and the pressure fighter closes in ominously and if the boxer fails to keep him at bay, he suffers little panic attacks. You can see it in that wide-eyed "uh-oh" look.

Pep walked blindly into the worst knockout loss of his career. He had no excuse. "I had won seventy-three fights in a row and I didn't think any kid named Sandy Saddler was going to beat me," he said. "I wasn't even a little worried."

Paulie walked into his knockout loss with eyes wide open. He doesn't need an excuse. He simply "bit off more than he could chew again," said Jeffrey Freeman of *KO Digest*. In fighting a younger, stronger, stylistic nightmare, he did what few million-dollar fighters would dare to do and he didn't blink. (Even Sugar Ray Robinson blinked when it came to Murderers' Row. He ran out on written contracts to meet two of them, avoided another one for years, and he did it during his breathtaking prime.) "You know who I was rewarded with in my first title fight?" he said last June, *"Miguel Cotto."*

And it hasn't been much easier since. He's been what Vegas calls an underdog with fleas. The odds were 12-5 against him when he faced Ricky Hatton, 4-1 when he faced Juan Diaz, and 5-1 when he faced Amir Khan. Vyacheslav Senchenko was undefeated and a 4.5-1 favorite when Paulie stopped him, but the handicappers scoffed and chalked him in as a 15-1 underdog when he faced the untested Adrien Broner. Paulie scoffed right back. "This is how the creation of Adrien Broner happened," he said before their bout. "They got everybody that's wrong for boxing together in one room, did everything that's wrong for boxing in that room, and gave birth to Adrien Broner." The sweet science, he told the press, requires more than talent at the upper level. Then he proceeded to prove it over twelve rounds. So then what happens? He signs to meet a fading Zab Judah, is once again declared an underdog, and dominates the rounds with a jab.

In January, Paulie said he was willing to fight Porter, despite the fact that no one else was calling out that beast. "What do you see in Porter that you can capitalize on?" he was asked. "I'm not saying I see any weaknesses," Paulie said. *You don't necessarily have to see a weakness in them to want to fight them.*" (emphasis mine)

When the smoke cleared Saturday night, it looked as if the roof fell on him. He may have regretted wanting to fight Porter. Now he's wondering what to do next. Retire? Face some plodding journeyman, look good, and retire a winner?

If he is not medically cleared to fight again by a responsible authority, then he has no choice but to retire. If he is cleared and there is no increased risk of injury in the aftermath of his knockout, then he has several choices.

The ghost of Willie Pep points at one of them: Fight Porter again.

Pep had two tune-ups after his knockout loss. Paulie can fight a second-rate swarmer close to home and fight him safely: vary the speed, placement, and force of the jab, avoid the inside where Porter's strength sapped his, avoid mid-range where he is reduced to punchers' meat, and practice staying just off the perimeter to draw him out and then counter and circle off. "Keep on the go," was Pep's recommendation. "Keep him off balance." If Paulie and especially Paulie's legs feel good after ten rounds, he can turn his attention toward Porter and lobby for a rematch.

To most citizens and a few tin-belt titlists more interested in celebrity than glory, it might seem crazy. Why would Paulie challenge his stylistic foil a second time? Anyone who has been paying attention knows the answer.

Pep, haunted by Saddler, knew the answer. "We had a rematch," he said, "and you better believe I was ready for him. Most of the writers were picking Sandy but I was ready for him. I was dead set on beating him no matter what."

So what happened? "You could look it up," Pep used to say with a smirk.

If Paulie decides to hang up his gloves, he will go down in boxing history as a profile in courage. If he returns to full capacity and considers avenging the worst knockout loss of his career, he should fight Porter the way Pep fought and beat Saddler, then do better than Pep and retire.

April 25, 2014

A Wrinkle in Time

Three months ago, Bernard "The Alien" Hopkins raised his gnarled hand to fight the most dangerous light heavyweight on the planet. Many wondered why. Those who did so aloud found themselves rebuked by a serious man: "Have you been paying attention to my career?" I have. His career is a study in bootstrap pride and star-flung ambitions.

One of his ambitions is to surpass the achievements of the *Ursa Major* of geriatric pugilists, Archie Moore.

Twenty years ago he was a workman toiling in the long shadows of Roy Jones Jr. and James Toney. Few saw him for who and what he was. The truth of him was obscured by more than an executioner's hood or an alien mask. What is the truth of him? Ask him and you'll be in for mind-bending misdirection. He knows better than you do that words don't matter. The answer has been unveiled, gradually, since he lost the middleweight crown at the ripe old age of forty. It's in a remarkable campaign that saw him seize the light heavyweight crown at age forty-six, lose it at forty-seven, and spend the last seventeen months spanking top-ranked contenders twenty years his junior. But it's his decision to face Sergey "Krusher" Kovalev two months before turning fifty that would make Archie Moore tip his top hat.

"Alien vs. Krusher" was televised live from Atlantic City on HBO Saturday night. I wasn't about to watch it from the couch. I put on a suit and boarded an Amtrak train at Boston. First class seemed about right.

The fellow traveler I shared a space with was too riveted to an iPad to acknowledge my presence. He was watching a college football game, drinking Bloody Marys like my Camaro drinks gasoline, and cheering at turnovers with increasing bravura. Once, glancing up from Liebling's essays, I found him in a fighter's pose with his right fist cocked as if. He looked closer to fifty than I do, but probably knew not a whit about Bernard Hopkins and what he was risking and reaching for that very day.

My seat faced backwards, which gives sentimental sorts like me an unwelcome feeling of being pulled kicking and screaming into the future like a reluctant astronaut. I looked out the window at the things receding behind us. At Central Falls, Rhode Island a prison appeared, sprawled behind fences and great concentric circles of barbed wire. Hopkins history. At seventeen, he was convicted of armed robbery and his name became a number. Inmate #Y4145 spent five years at Pennsylvania's Graterford Prison thinking about life and all that comes with it. Archie Moore also did time after stealing seven dollars from a street car. Both counted those lost years as a turning point. Both found an older mentor inside, a necessary man who showed them the ropes and blessed the boxing ring and their place in it. "It was then that I made up my mind," Moore said. "There were two ways to go, you understand, and only two." One was surrender and single file between cinderblocks. The other was hope and what Moore called "the glass mountain." Hopkins knows what that is. Many who came out of big-city housing projects will tell you it's the black man's experience —two steps up to slide four steps down, scratching and clawing in a desperate effort "to touch that peak with outstretched fingertips."

Moore and Hopkins made vows to climb.

It took years, but they proved their mettle as men and champions, and they wouldn't let the formative past recede out of reach. They made it a point to visit reform schools and penitentiaries to place a strong hand on the shoulders of outcasts. They brought hope. In the early 1990s, Hopkins actually held a training camp at Graterford. "I've seen how Bernard inspires the inmates," a promoter said. "I've seen their eyes light up. After sparring, he'll sit down and talk to them for hours."

I had a five-hour train ride to think about the fight and all that comes with it. Images strangely fitting flashed by the window. Military trucks and other *objets de la guerre* at ease in Pawtucket and rubble strewn along the tracks in Providence called to mind the Russian puncher. Antique tractors of no use to anyone anymore, half sunk in the ground. Somewhere near New Haven I saw cars piled like metal corpses in a dirt morgue, tires stripped, hoods open-mouthed. Only the graffiti had vitality. It flickered and then rushed by as the train crossed New York City's limits. Some of the tags took on a power of suggestion a subtle-minded theorist like Hopkins would not miss: "Solo," "Shock," "Bard," "Stoic," "Distort," "Duzzit," "Ready." One was not so subtle. Toward the end of a sun-splashed tunnel, twenty feet of sharp angles and pastel green went racing by that read "Alien Intelligence."

It got my hopes up.

In 1952, A.J. Liebling boarded this train at Penn Station on his way to cover Jersey Joe Walcott's world title defense against Rocky Marciano in Philadelphia. Across the aisle from him was a contingent of Brocktonians laying five-to-one odds on their hero. "They might have been either union officials or downtown businessmen," he observed. They were on the train with me, sixty-two years later, only the subject was less stirring than a championship bout and less historic than Hopkins's battle against two destroyers in Time and Kovalev. "The Eagles lose their quarterback. The Giants can't get out of their own way," said one. "They're supposed to have this lightning-quick offense and they're fumbling on their own line!" said another. I yawned.

At 4:10 p.m. I disembarked with Liebling's book where Liebling did at Philadelphia's 30th Street Station. Before boarding the

New Jersey Transit to Atlantic City, I scanned the concourse for some tribute to Hopkins, and found one, though it was a memorial to other warriors from a greater war. "Angel of the Resurrection" by Walker Hancock features a forty-foot bronze archangel holding up a fallen soldier. It was dedicated in August 1952. Liebling waddled past it only a month later on his way to the Municipal Stadium where he would witness "old man Walcott" collapse at Marciano's feet. In September of 1955, he would witness the Old Mongoose himself in the same undignified position. Both fell and could not get up.

At 12:11 a.m. I saw Youth deck Age yet again when Kovelev slung a right hand like an iron ball on a chain. It landed, literally and figuratively, on the temple of the Philadelphian.

But the Philadelphian got up.

Flying Objects

Kovalev's tendency to sling first and think later was tempered by a masterful strategy. He began with a statement of power to keep Hopkins at bay. It worked. After Hopkins was decked in round one, he adjusted his distance from the perimeter (only a half-step away from Kovalev's chin) to just off the perimeter (a full step outside Kovalev's reach). This adjustment was made early and told the story of the fight.

By round five, his trainer knew what was happening. He saw very human impulses of self-preservation. "You're not trusting your weapons," he told Hopkins in the corner. "Relax, get inside, and smother." But Hopkins could not relax and had no inclination for close encounters of any kind. Kovalev only had to feint to send thirty years of drills into complete disarray. Jabs likewise forced the thinking veteran to think again while a debilitating body attack depleted his already suspect energy reserves. What had been well-timed invasions against lesser opponents became infrequent forays against Kovalev. He seemed content to hover.

Hopkins later noted Kovalev's strategy of stepping out of range after landing his punches, though there was more to it. When Kovalev wasn't stepping back, he was finishing his combinations with a left hook or a jab. It's called "finishing on your left" and Marciano's trainer recommended it because it naturally returns the conventional fighter to the ready position. It does something else too: a left 'going away' is a surprise to opponents. A big right at the end of a combination registers as an exclamation point, a signal that the worst is over, and most fighters will follow it with their own attack. They don't expect a left to pop them on the nose. Not even Hopkins could figure it out.

Plan B from Outer Space

Hopkins had to reconfigure his whole motherboard. As winning became more and more remote, his objective was reduced and he found new answers to new questions. He would do what neither Walcott nor Moore could do against Marciano. He would go the distance. Kovalev, who had yet to stand around in his own sweat after twelve or even ten rounds waiting for judges' scorecards to be read, would have to tonight. Hopkins switched into defensive overdrive and displayed a vast array of old ring foils to find an advantage. In the third round he landed a left hook to the body and at the same time swung his right foot behind Kovalev's front foot, jammed his forearm under Kovalev's armpit, and pushed him down. Then he raised his hands in hopes that the referee would take the cue and start a count. It was an underhanded version of the Fitzsimmons Shift, which is over a century old.

In the eighth round, Hopkins was hurt by a right hand. He sagged and stumbled like a septuagenarian in a stairwell —and what does he do? He glances down at the canvas. It was a ploy, an ingenious one at that, to stunt Kovelev's adrenalin-fueled rush with a suggestion that perhaps, just perhaps, he'd slipped.

In the tenth round Hopkins surprised everyone. He gritted his dentures and landed a right blast that repeated all the way to the nosebleeds. Kovalev's leg shuddered and the Russians seated near me jumped up and spilled their vodka. *"Rossiya! Ataka!"* they hollered as their hero resumed control of the bout.

Bernard Hopkins finished the fight going toe-to-toe with Time the Destroyer and getting the worst of it. The crowd roared. I saw the glass mountain. I saw an old black man scratching and clawing in a desperate effort to touch that peak with outstretched fingertips.

It was 3:26 a.m. Sunday when the New Jersey Transit pulled into Philadelphia's 30th Street Station. Eleven hours earlier, I hadn't noticed its magnificence as a work of architecture. A coffered ceiling looms a hundred feet overhead and six Corinthian columns stand at the main entrances. The design of the building combines Neoclassicism with Art Deco, old with new.

With two hours to kill before the arrival of my Boston-bound train, I lingered with the low echoes in the main concourse. The chandeliers were dimmed and it was almost deserted. Spectral shoes clacked now and then on marble floors. An off-duty conductor was stretched out on a bench, snoring like three men in a chamber.

I wandered underneath Walker Hancock's war memorial and was reading the inscription when I sensed a presence over my shoulder. An old man stood there gazing up at the angel and the fallen warrior. I didn't hear him approach. His skin was the color of good coffee; gray mutton chops graced his face. He was smiling, as if he knew the answers. And then he was gone.

November 13, 2014

"Jack Demsey's"

New York. Late Friday afternoon I was walking along West 33rd Street thinking about how Bryant Jennings should fight Wlad Klitschko when I did a double-take. One of those dime-a-dozen joints in Midtown Manhattan has a name that still packs the proverbial wallop. The sign said "Jack Demsey's."

It takes a blink or two before you realize the "p" is missing.

Jack Dempsey's Restaurant, the real thing, used to be at 1619 Broadway. For thirty-six years (1938-1974), "The Manassa Mauler" greeted patrons, posed for Polaroids, and startled newcomers with a voice that was nothing like the growl they'd expected. "Hiya pal" he'd chirp, but when his oversized hand clasped yours, you knew. Those oversized hands earned him another moniker in his day —"Jack the Giant Killer." Despite standing a little over six feet and weighing less than a cruiserweight, it took him not one round to land a punch to the solar plexus that left six feet four inches of Carl Morris writhing on the canvas. It took not one round before Fred Fulton's seconds had to drag all six feet six dead-to-the-world inches of him back to the corner. And then came Jess Willard, boxing's first super-heavyweight champion. Dempsey greeted him with violence so visceral it remains disturbing to watch even today.

Violence saturates New York City's history like a blood-soaked towel. From the 1960s into the 1990s when Mayor Rudy Giuliani looked behind crime's curtain to see all those broken windows that needed repairing, the city was seething and unsafe. In 1969,

Dempsey himself was the target of an attempted mugging in Manhattan, but he flattened both of his attackers. He was seventy-four. "I just let 'em lie there and walked away," he said.

Things have calmed down since, gotten good even, though visitors find out the hard way that the city's aggression is innate. It's on the avenues where countless yellow cabs dart like fireflies night and day; in the pitched-forward posture of drivers leaning on horns and glowering through windshields; on the sardine sidewalks where stopping to tie your shoe can earn you a piledriver with no apology. In NYC, everyone is Dempsey.

Early Saturday evening, I was walking along East 33rd Street toward Madison Square Garden and thinking again about how Bryant Jennings should fight Wlad Klitschko when a loud type standing on the corner at Seventh Avenue almost impaled my shoe with a sirloin steak sign he was thumping on the pavement. "Kleetschko! Kleetschko! Kleetschko!" he said as he cut the air with bargain-bin jabs.

He was spreading the news. Klitschko's defense of his world heavyweight crown that night was billed as "The Champion Returns." That sounded even better after a couple of blinks. See, whenever the Ukrainian giant defends against a Great American Hope, I tend to wonder if Dempsey will show up.

Ukrainians and Ukrainian Americans showed up all right. They filled the Garden's nosebleed sections and decorated them with a sea of blue and yellow flags. During the preliminaries two zealous fans tried to drape a big one over the partition of the corridor where the fighters walk to the ring. They flung up the far corners like a couple would a picnic blanket in Central Park, but it floated down over a stern-faced cop whose hands flew up as he spun around. The couple retreated under his New York glower.

Former champions and celebrities promenaded by the cop as the main event got near. Rudy Giuliani showed up too. I turned around and saw Prince Charles Martin, an American heavyweight prospect who broke an Englishman's nose in a preliminary bout. "How would you fight Klitschko?" I asked him. He thought for a moment and said "I'd box him." Martin, who throws tricky shots from an upright stance, was shy about details. I suggested he watch the film of Dempsey-Willard and consider it a crash course in giant-toppling.

Jennings's eyes were wide as he made his way to the ring. I didn't see fear in them so much as confident awareness. He seemed to be in something of a meditative state. Minutes later the champion appeared with his entourage. His face was a mask of tension. Drenched with sweat, jaw clenched, pupils dilated; it was the face of Kiev or Peski between shellings. To his right a blue and yellow swarm rushed forward to let him know they were there. To his left was press row.

Klitschko's physical dimensions almost match Jess Willard's. The only notable difference between them is Willard's wrist, which was two and a half inches bigger than Klitschko's.

Before the end of the first round I thought Dempsey may have shown up after all. Jennings was showing agility and moving his head. He threw an overhand right from a low crouch, which the grand old champion identified as his favorite stance and one that is, he said, "invaluable in fighting bigger men." In the second round, Jennings was jabbing to the body and twisting his torso when Klitschko started throwing those telephone poles at him. Jennings responded by going low and springing into punches that sent the giant skittering away. In the fourth, he threw a whistling left hook followed by an overhand right that missed by an inch.

By then, Prince Charles Martin was no longer shy about details. He was hollering Dempsey-like directions behind me: "Make him fight! Step right into his space! Don't wait for him! Fire that right hand!"

Klitschko paused and took a deep breath in the fifth round. His objective is always the same —it's the same as Ukraine's. He seeks to control his territory. He jabs, he holds. He fires left hooks and right hands when it's safe to do so. Unlike Ukraine, if his opponent fires back, he'll clinch. And if he can't clinch, he'll make a fast exit, stage right, and try to reset the momentum. "Controlled panic," Jennings called it.

Jennings understands the problems presented by the giant. He was more effective than anyone expected in blocking, getting under and moving around the jab, and making Klitschko pay for clinches by banging his flanks. However, he wasn't banging nearly enough to win more than a few rounds, never mind the heavyweight championship of the world. Martin saw it. "Load that hook up!" he said during the ninth round. "Right hand over the top! Over the top!"

But Dempsey wasn't at the Garden Saturday night. According to CompuBox, Klitschko's head absorbed only twenty-six total punches over twelve rounds. Willard's head absorbed *thirty-six* power punches in the *first* round.

Bryant Jennings proved aggressive-ready, but not willing enough. His low crouch was a pose —like an old photograph in one of those dime-a-dozen joints around Midtown Manhattan— like Jack Demsey's.

April 27, 2015

The British in Boston

F*riday afternoon, at the weigh-in.* "I love the Boston accent," said a tourist behind me. We were standing on the sun-splashed cobblestones at Faneuil Hall as Mayor Marty Walsh officially welcomed big-time boxing back to the land of "Rocky Mahciano, Tony DeMahco, and Mahvelous Mahvin Haglah."

A few minutes later, fighters scheduled to compete on the undercard of Premier Boxing Champions' "Dirrell vs. DeGale" show at Agganis Arena were herded out, stripped down, and stood like Adonises in their underwear. "This is so cool!" said a co-ed as she whipped out her Galaxy and starting snapping pictures. Beside her was someone I supposed was her beau, looking a little blanched. I wondered if she was secretly zooming in.

About fifty English fans were on hand to support London's James DeGale. They mixed with the curious foot traffic that had stalled by the stage, under old Sam Adams's statue. They were easy to spot. All of them wore T-shirts that said "Team Chunky" and almost all of them were wavering in the breeze. "My head's on ff*cking fffire," said one of them as he took a long drag from a cigarette. "Where's our next pub?"

I looked around for a T-shirt that was standing steady and soon found one. I asked him why DeGale, a broad-shouldered athlete and rising contender in the *Transnational Boxing Rankings*, happened to be called "Chunky." "Ask his sister," he said and gestured toward a young woman standing nearby. Eloise DeGale has a gold complexion with features perfectly formed. Her eyes can melt a man's heart, or drill a hole in it. I hadn't finished asking her whether James was chunky when he was a boy when his opponent went wading past, followed by members of his entourage. "The champ is here!" said one of them. The drunk contingent grumbled at that. "DeGale" they said. Andre Dirrell's man turned around. "De Girl? De Girl?" he said, laughing. "De Chump!"

"—James was fat," Eloise said, ignoring him.

"Is that the reason he got himself to a gym?" I asked again. It wasn't.

"He had a lot of energy," she said, "and was headed down the wrong path. Boxing changed his direction, love."

At my left, Dirrell changed *his* direction and was wading furiously back through the crowd. His voice rose above the din like a musket shot. "Who's smoking?! Who's smoking!?"

"Who do you think will win?" Eloise asked. "DeGale," I admitted. "But let's not spread that around. I don't want to have to bop my way outta here—"

Only a stone's throw away is State Street. It used to be called King Street before we changed it to emphasize a point. It was the site of an incident that united Boston against the British crown a few years before the American Revolution. When the smoke cleared one day in 1770, five colonists lay dead or dying after a small contingent of Redcoats opened fire. That incident is remembered as "The Boston Massacre" but that wasn't what it was. It began as a series of bad interactions between soldiers and resentful locals and was provoked into something worse by drunken rowdies itching for a fight. Old Sam Adams recast a riot into an execution of innocents and shoved his country toward a war we were lucky to win.

The latest British invader called "Chunky" weighed in at 167.2 pounds. Angry Andre Dirrell, this afternoon's Crispus Attucks, clenched his teeth and ripped off his shirt and his abdominals looked like the cobblestones we were standing on, like the cobblestones Attucks landed on when he fell backward in a heap with two holes in his chest. Dirrell weighed in at 167.8. The English heckled

him and he provoked them further by pointing his finger and slowly
scanning the crowd with it. Eloise laughed and did the same in mock
disco. At the customary stare-down, he got a little too close and
jawed a little too much. DeGale, more professional, wore the Union
Jack around his bare shoulders.

While on my way to catch the Green Line at Park Street station,
I overheard a local tour guide addressing a crowd at the entrance of
Boston Common. "British soldiers camped only steps from where
we stand. You can imagine the offense...."

Saturday afternoon, at the main event. In the second round, DeGale's
offense sent the angry American falling backwards in a heap. It was
a perfectly timed overhand that did it, and it was set up by a loitering
jab that blinded Dirrell just long enough. Dirrell got up immediately
and began jawing all over again though at whom and for what was
anyone's guess. He was knocked down a second time and when the
bell finally ended the longest round of his life, he was on his knees.
I don't think he fully regained consciousness until about the fifth
round.

Dirrell was fighting like an over-drilled soldier loading and re-
loading a musket. The Englishman did to him what we did to En-
glishmen in 1776 —he circled, bluffed, fired and retreated, then fired
again from treetops and from around corners. Every consonant in
his attack was relaxed, his performance smoothed out. While Dirrell
marauded desperately and clunked about, DeGale flowed in and out
like the easy tide.

Rodney "The Punisher" Toney, a top-ten middleweight exactly
twenty years ago this month, sat beside me. He was watching the
fight closely, musing to himself about what he would have done
with DeGale. "He's smooth. I woulda made it ugly," he said. "That's
what I did." As Dirrell's chances of winning ebbed away, the crowd
starting chanting "USA! USA!" Toney, a provocateur from the beginning, still sought to make it ugly. "USA gonna get whipped today!" he said.

But Dirrell roared back like a true patriot; I thought he won the fourth, seventh, ninth, and tenth rounds and had a few he didn't win marked close. Credit is due his corner for making sure the USA didn't get "whipped today." Among them was cut man Scott Rehm.

Rehm, forty-six, has a Boston backstory that rivals Sam Adams's. Already a combat sport veteran before he inexplicably became an MMA fighter at the age of forty, he got himself billed as "Sweet Dreams" and began knocking out guys half his age in a minute or less on the New England circuit. He'll tell you he was really a boxer who smoked too much to do ten rounds, so he brought his heavy hands to the cage, where he only had to do five. The losses on his record? He waves them off with a laugh. They only happened when he got "tangled up." He has since become a formidable cut man in the UFC and boxing who studies the craft and the history of the craft like few others this side of Stitch Duran.

Dirrell ended up losing a unanimous decision, but blood and bumps had nothing to do with it and that means Rehm did his job. He found me in the cheap seats during the walkout bout. I told him it looked like he had eight arms wiping down Dirrell, slipping out his mouthpiece, stuffing the Q-tip up his bloody nose, applying Enswell to his forehead and ice to his chest, greasing him, slipping in the mouthpiece.

"Everything went smoothly," he said.

I had, however, noticed something amiss in both corners. The arena had supplied them with flimsy aluminum stools with the seat screwed onto a single pole. "Everything went smoothly, except for that," Rehm said again. "At the end of the ninth, I climbed into the ring and when they handed me the stool, I put it down and the damn top fell off."

He said he shot his hand up to Dirrell's back "—Don't sit!"

May 25, 2015

The Hyannis Fight Crowd

I was standing outside the Hyannis Youth and Community Center, eavesdropping. "Dude, I never saw a live boxing match in my life," said someone to my left. He was holding a plastic cup and wore a beard and a baseball cap, today's uniform for twenty-something white guys. One of two others around him took a sip and bonded. "Me neither dude," he said, looking away. "—But Barboza's gonna kick his azz!" All three caps nodded eagerly at that, like duck bills at Wonder Bread.

Hyannis, Massachusetts is the commercial hub of a peninsula that sinks about six inches into the Atlantic every summer when vacationers pour in from all over New England and New York. The Cape Cod demographic is old, white, and rich; lots of widows. "Barboza" is one of only nine hundred or so African Americans living in Hyannis (total population: fourteen thousand). He is a graduate of Barnstable High School and, said the baseball cap boys, "the best running back in BHS history." He's a boxer now, with "Bad News" as a *nom de guerre* though the "News" is strictly local. All twelve of his professional bouts have been in Rhode Island or Massachusetts and his appearance in last night's main event was only two miles from his alma mater.

Forty dollars was good for a general admission ticket. I got mine in the mail. The fight crowd here has all the usual characters and then some: there were college kids looking for a thrill, roughnecks, bodybuilders with spray-on tans (one wore a T-shirt that read "Not

Even Flexing"), tattooed blondes on parade, a smattering of old salts, and a few families indulging dad's passion. Enough African Americans joined a strong Latino presence to turn Hyannis's racial distribution on its head, and yet there was none of the self-enforced segregation we've come to expect watching CNN and no one gave the cops on detail a hard time. In fact, everyone seemed to know each other. Bro-hugs were happening all around when the announcer climbed into the ring.

"...For the first time in nearly a decade, boxing returns to Cape Cod!"

That got them out of their seats in the bleachers, where I sat shoulder-to-shoulder with a couple of Cape Verdeans and two black women thumbing through Bayberry catalogs. Behind me to the right was a pocket-size Mexican called Mario. He had the big hands of a bricklayer and his bad English didn't prevent him from making gentlemen's bets all night.

The announcer invited the crowd to stand for the national anthem and handed the microphone to a well-groomed vocalist. Someone yelled "Take yah hat off!" and two hats in the front rows disappeared quick as a flash. I saw Tony DeMarco, the welterweight champion when the title was singular and singularly meaningful, standing straight and true under the flag. The vocalist, a tenor whose perfect hair would be standing on end in another minute, cleared his throat. *"Oh, say can you see by the dawn's early light, what so proudly we hailed at the twilight's last gleaming?* [—so far so good.] *Whose broad stripes and bright stars* [—he sounded a lot better than Jamie Foxx did at Mayweather-Pacquiao last spring] *thru the perilous fight* ...." He forgot the lyrics. Panic's silent wave stiffened him and bugged his eyes and he decided to just end it. *"And the hommmme of the buhraaaaave!"*

Everyone noticed but no one laughed until the Bayberry ladies in front of me let out a couple of guffaws that kept on coming. One of them finally caught her breath and said, "This is gonna be a good night!"

It was.

A welterweight bout opened the show. The two fighters had one win between them and a combined total of thirteen losses. During the introductions, Mario tapped the shoulder of one of the Cape Verdeans. "Who you got?"

Malik Jackson, from Newark, wore trunks that said "Freaky Deaky" and immediately started swapping punches with Hartford's Oscar Diaz. Diaz, who hasn't won a fight yet, obliged him and landed a good shot then fell into a clinch to chill the counter. When he saw a lot of mouths agape in the crowd over Jackson's shoulder, he made a face that said "How'd yah like that?" but lost ground in the next round. In the third, Jackson hit him with a right that sent him jangling into the ropes. He wound up and threw three more that Diaz blocked before inexplicably dropping his hands and mugging at Jackson. He never saw the right hook whistling in. We heard the smack of wet leather in the bleachers and all expression left Diaz's face. Jackson was winding up a sixth one as Diaz leaned forward as if he were reading Jackson's trunks. The referee was out of position and couldn't save a limp-limbed Diaz from falling through the ropes and out of the ring. He fell in sections. Pitching forward, his rear end jutted out as he sank to a sitting position on the third rope, then his head jerked back and caught on the second rope and he was essentially slingshotted through and out. The last thing we saw as he disappeared from sight was his legs lifted in the air in mock victory.

It was, move for move, an exact reproduction of Jack Dempsey's famous plunge out of the ring at the hands of Luis Firpo. The difference for Diaz was that there were no typewriters to land on and no reporters to push him back into the ring. Ersatz Dempsey crash-landed on the floor. Medics, cops, and fans with iPhones rushed forward. My section was facing the spectacle and so could only hope the hell he didn't land on his head. "That shouldn't have happened! The ref is no good!" screamed the Bayberrys. A Cape Verdean to my right agreed. "That ref was about three punches late."

Then Diaz's head popped up, smiling. He got an ovation. Jackson figured it was for him and was up in the ring taking bows when he saw Diaz, realized his mistake, and started thumping his gloves together. Diaz, now 0-8, climbed back through the ropes and the two fighters embraced like long-lost brothers.

The second preliminary bout was between a welterweight and a super middleweight meeting in the middle. In the red corner was a fighter from New Jersey called "The Technician." He towered over a mixed martial artist from Brockton exploring more dangerous ground. Mario tapped me on the shoulder just before the first bell. "Who you got?" I told him I didn't know either one but would tell him in three minutes. After one I turned around. "I don't need three minutes. Brockton can't fight. I say The Technician, unless he gets caught with something stupid." And that's precisely what happened. Whenever my guy finished punching, he'd bring his fists back and leave his head dangling in range like a lame sparrow by a snake pit. Brockton winged something stupid and down went The Technician. In the second round, he got hit with something stupid again and down he went again. In the third, Brockton pinned him on the ropes and threw punches that came up from the floor and out from behind his back and there's The Technician slipping into every one. Mario won that bet.

Two white men in their early sixties, the Cape Cod demographic, were chattering behind me. I leaned back, eavesdropping again. "He has a family. Works all day landscaping and trains at night," one of them, Tim, said to the other, whose name is Russ. "He made forty thousand last year." They were talking about the popular Paul Gonsalves, who was scheduled next. Tim is a carpenter who used to work with Gonsalves, and has followed his career ever since. I did the math. Gonsalves had five fights last year. After you factor in the manager's cut, trainer's cut, travel and miscellaneous expenses, that's approximately $3536 per fight before taxes. Factor in a conservative estimate of hours in the gym over a month, and Gonsalves's hourly wage looks less than a skilled landscaper can expect on Cape Cod.

And landscapers don't get punched in the face.

Gonsalves was stopped in his last two fights but had it easy tonight. I don't recall him being punched at all by his opponent, one of two soft imports from Sonora, México.

Jose Humberto Corral, the second Mexican import brought in for tonight's card, was softer than the first but determined to do something about his 18-18 record. He fought a young cruiserweight from Pembroke, a bedroom community forty miles north of Hyannis. I was amused to know that Pembroke could produce a fighter, never mind one calling himself "the American Nightmare." The Nightmare was strong and aggressive, but I would have bet Mario my Camaro that Corral spent hours watching Roberto Duran on the USA network in the 1990s. In other words, he knew how to fight fat. When the well-muscled favorite barreled in, Corral would fade back and throw a slapping left hook. He slipped well, clinched well, went slack inside to steal a rest, and mounted the fat attack Duran perfected long ago: zing in combinations and left hooks to the body, step out of reach, and suck wind. Corral's right, however, was an insult to Duran; he threw it like Aunt Minnie. Still, he was trying.

When he came back to his corner after the first round, he stood for a moment scanning the crowd as if he wanted everyone to know that despite his record, he was vying for approval. I did what empathetic types do and applauded. Round two was an inspired one and I thought he won it. Winning it took plenty out of him. I noticed him pushing his mouthpiece out before the bell rang, which is a sure sign of fatigue. Before turning around to sit on the stool, he looked in our direction. The Bayberrys saw him and stood up to applaud. They're empathetic types too. "That's right! That's right!" they called out.

After the third round, he began reaching out his glove to the Nightmare as if to keep it friendly. Fatigue was making a coward out of him. Still, he kept himself safe by turning his head with punches and feinting a punch of his own to get his opponent to step back and buy himself a few extra seconds' rest. He wasn't trying to win anymore. The Nightmare got bolder and started landing harder and more often, and there's Corral nodding his head every time he did, as if he were a quality-control manager —"Yes, that landed. Yes, that hurt." The Bayberrys, who had tossed their catalogs aside during the aborted national anthem, were losing interest. "I like that white boy's socks," said one of them. "I'm gonna get some." Russ turned to Tim and said "The Thrilla in Manila this isn't." In the last minute of the bout, the fighters were at close quarters and Corral threw an overhand right that I still can't figure out. It looped up behind his own head and landed backwards with all the force of a scallop roll. The bell rang and Corral was joyous, despite the obvious loss. He jumped up on the ropes and instead of raising his arms like a winner or a winner of sorts, he made the sign of the cross like a relieved pilgrim.

"Mario," someone said to the gambler, "you won only one of four tonight." Mario mustered up an appalled look and waved two fingers in his face. "I won thdee! Thdee!" Then he looked at me and I looked at his two fingers and he looked at his two fingers and sheepishly flicked another one up. "Thdee!"

The crowd perked up when Hyannis's own "Bad News" Barboza appeared for the main event. Waiting for him in the ring was a rough-looking forty-year-old Pennsylvanian who supplements his income by getting knocked out by bigger and better fighters. He was brought in to contest some makeshift regional title called the Northeast Heavyweight Championship. "I don't think Barboza is going to show me anything I haven't seen before," he said at the weigh-in. One minute into the bout he was reduced to a pile of jutting limbs at Barboza's feet and proven correct.

A microphone was stuck in Barboza's face and he shouted "I love you all!" to his neighbors and friends.

On the way out, I stopped by Tony DeMarco's table where he was signing and selling his autobiography. "The once and forever welterweight champion," I told him. He laughed and grabbed my shoulder. "Everything good?" he said. He has a tough time remembering my name and I don't blame him.

"Steve?" he asked.

"Springs," I said.

"Strings?"

"Dude, imagine something like this in Vegas," said a new boxing fan as he pushed open a community center door. "Dude, it's different when you know someone," said his companion.

Fans were milling outside, gathered in little circles discussing the night's mayhem, smoking, reuniting with high school classmates. Many of them knew Gonsalves and Barboza. "Pfffft. A one-minute main event," scoffed one of them. "I'ma tell Barboza I want my money back." Someone cuffed him on the shoulder and said "Good luck with THAT!" A bent and towering black man with a white beard was among a group of sixty or seventy-somethings. "—Bareknuckle right here! Who wants it?" he said to a passing group of twenty-somethings. "Better get me before I go to sleep! It's past my bedtime." A pickup truck rolled by in the parking lot. A passenger hanging out the window with both hands raised was hollering "And the new! And the new!" It startled white beard. "I'm ready for you!" he hollered back. "I'm ready! I gotta bring my cane in the ring, though. Bareknuckle!" That got belly laughs from his friends. One of them saw he was unsteady and held the bend of his elbow.

Things quieted down. The crowd was drifting in different directions now, some had DeMarco's book tucked under an arm.

"We gotta get together like this more often," said one of the old-timers.

"We do."

"But you never call me!"

"Well, you know me!"

One of the last to leave was eighty-one-year-old George Maddox, who just may be the greatest boxer Cape Cod has ever produced. His right hand was clenched at his waist and he dragged his right foot as he walked. He was honored in the ring before the main event for his contributions to boxing and on behalf of the hundreds of

Hyannis youth whose lives he touched. When he spoke into the microphone he was facing the flag and DeMarco, who was standing under it. I couldn't hear what he said then, so I asked him as he was passing me.

"I was calling him out," he said.

"You were calling him out? Fifty-five years after your prime?" Maddox has lived in Hyannis since he was three. His parents brought him up from segregated Alabama during the Depression after migrating north to find work. Maddox was sixteen when he had his first recorded fight. It was on Main Street, a ten-minute walk from where we stood, and was broken up by a trainer named Clinton Perry, one of six Cape Verdean brothers who touched his life. "If you want to fight, go to the gym so you can stay out of trouble!" Perry told Maddox. That's just what he did. He trained at a gym on South Street and later at Joe Pete's Gym in Mashpee. As an amateur, he went 165-12, took several regional Golden Gloves titles and had what he'll tell you was "the great privilege of competing at Madison Square Garden." As a professional, he was a middleweight who could make the welterweight limit.

"DeMarco should have fought me," he said wistfully.

Paul Pender should have too. In August 1959, Maddox was in Providence, Rhode Island and scored a knockout on the same card that saw Paul Pender become the New England middleweight champion by beating "Sergeant" Jackson Brown. Maddox had been promised a shot at the winner. When he got the runaround, he went after Brown in January to make a point. "I annihilated him," Maddox said, "but Pender wouldn't fight me." Later that month, Pender defeated Sugar Ray Robinson and became the world middleweight champion.

"What is your fondest boxing memory?" I asked him.

"Sparring [Rocky] Marciano down at Grossinger's."

"Were you out of your mind?"

"I was afterwards!" he laughed. "No, they brought me in for speed. I was steering around him pretty good. One time he hit me on my arm and nearly broke it. He hit so hard. But what a nice man he was."

The biggest purse he earned was $688, though he trained as if thousands *were* at stake. In his mind, thousands were at stake—the faith of that many neighbors and friends on Cape Cod. He'd roll out of bed at four in the morning, drive to Craigville Beach in the dark, and run miles on the soft sand and then back along the shoreline. "Legs and wind," he told me. "It built up my legs and got me in great condition." He'd wear a beanie and a towel around his neck when he ran and recalled the time a police cruiser stopped him. "They thought I was running from a robbery with the loot!" he laughed. After that, they'd flash the blue lights at him out of respect.

They still do. A cop on detail approached us, embraced him, and asked about his wife, who has muscular dystrophy. Maddox, who suffered a stroke some years ago, credits his roadwork with keeping him in shape enough to take care of her. "Can we give you a lift home?" the cop asked. Maddox declined and said something about opening up more boxing gyms in Hyannis "to put you fellas out of business." "You won't hear me complaining!" said the cop over his shoulder.

It was getting late. I said good night and began walking away when another question came to mind and I turned around. The old pro was a study in classic form and human dignity as he made his way to his car; it was parked on the other side of the now-empty parking lot, in the corner. I watched and every question was answered. Stepping with his left foot, dragging his right foot —the fighter he once was and forever is, pressing on.

August 9, 2015

Peu Exposés

The undercard of HBO Pay-Per-View's "Gennady 'Triple G' Golovkin vs. David Lemieux" was underway when someone behind me got bored watching a Bahamian bounce an Irishman off the canvas. "What's the second 'G' in 'Triple G' for?" he asked.

"Goliath," said a wit.

"Golem," said another.

The third 'G', "Golovkin," sounds to me like something big under a bridge in a Grimm's fairy tale or one of J.R.R. Tolkien's early draft names for Morgoth, the Dark Lord of the North.

Madison Square Garden was loud and restless and sold out. A final tally of twenty thousand, five hundred and forty-eight was gathering around the ring and from my vantage point those entertaining any notion that the French-Canadian slugger, Lemieux, could win were in the single digits. One of them was spotted in section one, row sixteen; he was turned around conversing with row seventeen.

"Who you here for?" a New Yorker in row eighteen said, leaning forward.

"Well, I am Canadian."

"Bet me a hun'ed, right here," the New Yorker said as he made a show of reaching into his pocket.

"I'm sorey" said the Canadian. "I have two hundred on Lemieux already. I'd rather not lose three hundred."

The New Yorker, expecting an edge for an edge, had geared up for an argument that never came. He muttered something under his breath and scanned the area for a live one. A live one soon ambled by looking for row eighteen. He squeezed in, perilously balancing a beer and spilling popcorn and was greeted thus: "You must be for Lemieux. You have his hair!" Indeed he did. He wore glasses, but his head was shaved on the sides and the mohawk in the middle was greased flat just like the underdog tonight. "Not me," laughed the new arrival, who turned out to be Polish.

The New Yorker muttered again and turned to the action. The Bahamian was still planting leather all over the panting Irishman in the ninth round. "Finish him already!" he said. "Take a dive!" That got laughs and he sat back, satisfied.

I was two seats down from Lemieux's double. Between us sat a clean-cut Puerto Rican named Kelvin whose favorite fighter is Wilfredo Gomez. "What do you think?" I asked him about the main event. "Golovkin will go to the body," he said. "And Lemieux will be finished in seven or eight rounds. The ref will save him." I saw it a little differently. "The onus is on Lemieux's trainers," I said. "If they don't have a good strategy and a contingency plan or two, he hasn't a chance." The size difference was nothing to ignore either. Lemieux was listed at five feet nine. Golovkin at five ten and a half. But those numbers must be off; Golovkin is noticeably bigger than Lemieux, whose low-crouch stance makes him smaller still.

"There he goes," Kelvin nudged me and pointed down toward the ring. "Lemieux." I strained and saw a figure curving through the crowd like an otter through an eddying brook. Instead of heading from the side entrance to the dressing room, Lemieux was making a show of his self-confidence like the New Yorker did reaching into his pocket to bet against him.

Midnight approached and by then Lemieux had rested, dressed, warmed up, and was in the ring. A minute later Tolkien's dark lord walked down the aisle, resplendent in an ornate robe. When the two fighters faced each other during the referee's instructions, someone stood up and shouted, "Get the body bag ready!"

The Canadians, subdued by their native disposition and perhaps by the pandemonium around them, were quiet. They held their flags so low they might have been handkerchiefs; one had hands folded around hers as if in prayer.

When the bell rang, all eyes fell on Lemieux as he hard-stepped out of his corner. Would he barrel at the most feared fighter in the world to make a point? He would and did and ran into a jab, which was of the cramming, not the flicking kind. It travelled from mid-range –trainers call it "the puncher's range"– where the fully extended arm stretches about a foot behind the target's head. That range, combined with Golovkin's heavy hands, transformed a simple set-up punch into a debilitating weapon. And it came again and again.

I was reminded of another middleweight, Hall of Famer Ken Overlin who fought hard-punching Al Hostak, also at Madison Square Garden in 1941. "When I started working on him," he said afterward, "his head kept bobbing back as if he was nodding 'hello' to everyone in the house."

The second round was a snapshot of the whole fight. Lemieux threw a left hook that missed, then weaved under and to his left in anticipation of a right-hand counter. But Golovkin wasn't there. He had stepped back, and that tell-tale step dashed whatever chance Lemieux thought he had. Golovkin was letting on that he would not get into a mindless shootout with the slugger; he would jab him silly, apply ominous psychological pressure, feint him out of position, and capitalize on every flaw. I noticed one of them: Lemieux was holding his guard high with his elbows in front of his flanks. Golovkin noticed it too and landed hooks to those flanks. Lemieux dropped his elbows immediately to his sides and retreated to the ropes, a concession he tried to rescind by reversing direction and unadvisedly hurling himself nose-first into another ramrod jab. By then his mohawk was flying up so regularly it became a cue for ring-side photographers to start snapping.

Late in the round, he complained about being hit on the back of the head. He was looking for help. It was the second of what would be a succession of similar signals, *peu exposés*. In the third round, Golovkin hit him with a left hook high on the ribs —and he nodded. He put his guard up and Golovkin split it with two jabs and then began another assault which compelled Lemieux to do what sluggers never do unless they are overpowered —he held on. It was the fourth signal in the first nine minutes. Lemieux's quiet desperation was leaking out.

A left hook in round four sent him staggering, glassy-eyed. Again, his guard shot up and again Golovkin's jab battered through it. Lemieux tried ducking under what was coming next, but Golovkin's right hook was a scythe in a downward arc and it landed anyway. He retreated to the ropes and motioned for Golovkin to come closer with feigned bravado. When Golovkin obliged, Lemieux tried neither to counter nor clinch, and merely circled away. I turned to Kelvin and said "so much for strategy; he has none." Golovkin was looking more and more like a middleweight Michael Myers, "Triple M." At the end of the round, Lemieux smiled sheepishly at Golovkin, who wore a mask of brutal indifference.

Lemieux went down in the fifth round. It was a left hook to the body that did it. And then Golovkin, who is drilled to throw a right hand after a left hook (and a left hook after a right hand) hit him with exactly that while Lemieux was crouching like Jamie Lee Curtis in the closet. It was an illegal blow. The Canadian in row sixteen turned around, visibly flustered. "What do you think aboat that? Should Triple G be disqualified?" Lemieux's quiet desperation had gone public. "It wasn't intentional," I said. "He's on automatic."

When Lemieux landed a left hook on Golovkin's chin in the sixth round, it shook him for a second. Didn't Curtis stick a coat hanger in the eyes of her monster? It almost wasn't worth it. Golovkin began toying with him, throwing lead uppercuts, and smashing his nose into a red smear. Even so, Lemieux never stopped trying, even as his face began to come apart and his spirit wilted. In the seventh, the referee was concerned enough to halt the action and summon the physician to the ring apron. "I'm okay! I'm okay!" Lemieux said. I leaned over in my seat, looking past Kelvin and Lemieux's double to find the New Yorker standing up.

At one minute and thirty-three seconds into the eighth round, the drama show ended and Kelvin's prediction proved not only astute but eerily accurate. Lemieux had gotten too close and Golovkin, slashing away, missed a right hand and followed up with a left hook that crashed into Lemieux's right upper abdominopelvic quadrant —his liver. Rows sixteen, seventeen, and eighteen stood up.

Have you ever been hit like that by a professional boxer? I have. It makes whatever they do in the MMA a springtime dalliance. It can give you instant PTSD. The worst thing about it isn't the pain, it's the cruel delay *before* the pain. You get just enough time to think about it; two seconds of panic that unmans the roughest and the toughest. Most guys try vainly to muffle a bellow that sounds like a gutted steer, though I recall squeaking once. A heavyweight contender in the 1990s was hit with just such a hook and said it made him fart all over the ring.

Lemieux gritted his teeth. Then he turned purple and folded inward, momentarily forgetting the live danger in front of him. And, despite self confidence that only began to fray twenty-five minutes earlier when the first hook struck his flank, despite his drive to beat the odds and become the best, despite his many victories, months of training and years spent steeling his resolve, he signaled his surrender: as he stumbled backward, he turned his head and looked at the referee. It was just a glance, but the referee saw it for what it was and jumped in to rescue him.

"What'd Lemieux say to the ref?" someone behind me asked.

"Help me," I said.

October 22, 2015

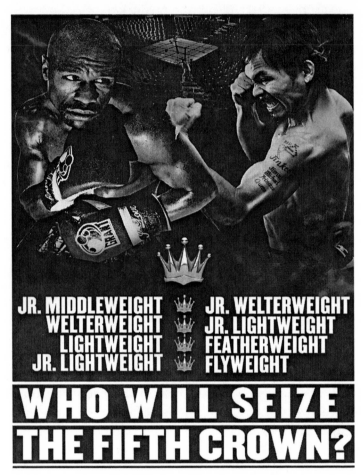

Created by Cameron Burns

MAY-PAC REDUX

Thunderstruck

AC/DC's "Thunderstruck" blared as Manny Pacquiao made his way to the ring with his entourage. Two giants walked behind him. On the left was Michael Moorer, former light heavyweight contender and history's first southpaw heavyweight champion now operating as the chief assistant trainer at the Wild Card Gym in Hollywood. On the right was the professional wrestler David Bautista, a half-Filipino known as "The Animal." Trainer Freddie Roach's prediction that Manny would stop Ricky Hatton inside of three rounds was a whisper on everyone's mind. Pacquiao himself provided the contrast to these ominous sounds and images. He smiled his boyish smile, stepped into the ring, and went immediately to the corner to get down on his knees and pray.

As it was, the fanfare was entirely appropriate. And Roach was right. With exactly eight seconds left in the second round, Pacquiao threw a dummy right jab, got low while weaving slightly to his left and launched a left hook that slammed into the side of Hatton's chin. It landed at the short angle, forcing the chin into the raised left shoulder and collapsing Hatton like the Scarecrow on Yellow Brick Road. Unconsciousness was immediate, his head hit the canvas, his lungs heaved for breath, and his eyes stared at something far away. We've seen it many times. It ain't pretty.

The punch that did it approached the aesthetic, however. Its execution and effect were about as devastating as any shot that we've seen in a heavily-promoted fight since Hearns's lullaby lasers. Indeed, round thirteen in Marciano-Walcott I and round five in Robinson-Fullmer II may have competition for their respective claims of "the perfect punch." At the very least, from this point forward no great knockout compilation will be complete without round two of Pacquiao-Hatton.

At the first bell, Hatton came out of his corner like a landlord coming out of his house with a shotgun. For a few seconds, Pacquiao behaved like a trespasser caught in the line of fire. He backed off, stepped away to the side and out of range, and threw tentative punches. He seemed a bit jittery. He settled down soon enough and began applying strategy — looping right hooks (not straight lefts as expected) at Hatton's chin.

Like an agitated landlord, Hatton's aggression wasn't quite the thinking type. He came out of his house armed, but in a straight line. And that was the least of his errors. Hatton was dropping his hands despite his corner's exhortations to keep his hands up, and his head was statue-still. Hatton's most elemental fault is that he tends to fight *tensely*. He grits his teeth and clenches his muscles and has never learned to fight with fluidity, to be loose. When he tries, it's forced and lasts only as long as stress is low. Fighters like this are prone to shatter. This is why we pack cookie jars in bubble wrap. It's why your car has shock absorbers. We can't wrap our chins in bubble wrap or attach shock absorbers to our necks, but we can roll with punches and fight in a relaxed manner to decrease the risk of getting knocked out.

Meanwhile, loose and fluid Manny was throwing arcing shots from a crouch and was timing the stronger man. Five of the southpaw's right hooks landed in the first two minutes.

The sixth right hook that connected in the first round was thrown as Hatton was throwing his own left hook. Pacquiao landed his as he went under Hatton's and then immediately spun off to his right and resumed position to punch. Hatton's whizzing hook looked like the propeller of a crashing helicopter, accelerating him down to the canvas. He got up at the count of eight. At the end of the round, he went down again from a straight left. He was trained to expect straight lefts and was surprised by the rapid-fire variety, unexpected angles, and the force of impact.

Manny Steward observed something else during the furious assault. Pacquiao was demonstrating the ability to combine offense and defense simultaneously. This is rare for an aggressive fighter. It is less rare for a great fighter. In his prime, Roberto Duran was able to do this masterfully due to superb training and surprising agility. Neither Manny's technique nor his beard is as full as Duran's, though his agility, ferocity, and use of angles are indeed comparable. His resume is on track to do the same. Incidentally, Duran had a timeless nickname: the Hands of Stone. Perhaps Manny should get his nickname out of the 1980s. If he cannot get timeless he can at least get modern; after all, he doesn't just eat up his opponents like Pacman, he gets downright "Matrix" in how he does it.

Dropped twice and stunned more than a few times, Hatton was glassy-eyed but kept on coming. I kept thinking of the metaphorical landlord. It turned out that the metaphorical trespasser had three guns to his one and was shooting him to pieces right there on his own front lawn. The landlord, hurt and bewildered, was still coming. He had to —it's his house. He had to; even though he knew in his heart of hearts he wasn't going to win this.

At the end, Hatton was out cold for well over a minute. Laid out on his lawn. He regained his senses and left without being interviewed. As I watched him leave the ring, I could almost hear King Levinsky (who lasted less than a round against Joe Louis) offer his own insights about being knocked out: "It's not the blows, much as they hurt... it's all them witnesses. Everybody watching you. You split to pieces, like a goddamn plate glass window hitting the sidewalk."

The look on Hatton's face as he departed was a mixture of dejection and embarrassment. I'd like to suggest to him that he should be neither. He has far less flaws as a man than he does as a fighter and that's something to aspire to. He has reminded us all that the best nobility is found among the working classes, among those who laugh at themselves, who'd die for their family, and who make their way by the sweat of their brow and the camaraderie of friends. He is a champion familiar with glory and only recently introduced to defeat. He is a man who did not go gently to that introduction.

Hatton should be encouraged to keep a proper perspective. He lost but one house last night. He will never lose his home, for his home is in the hearts of thousands, plus one, who sing of his heroism —even as he falls.

May 2, 2009

Flim Flam Floyd

A fool and his money. . .
—Benjamin Frankin

According to a reliable witness who must remain anonymous, any bills Floyd Mayweather Jr. is waving around these days are Monopoly money.

Floyd, it is alleged, was the victim of a swindle, a bunko, a flim-flam. He got conned.

A "con" or "confidence trick" is an operation where a swindler identifies a potential victim (a "mark") and gains the trust of that person. A person of means, particularly the gullible type, is a mouth-watering mark. Often, an inside man or a decoy is on the scene to vouch for the swindler, but just as often confidence is won after an initial or "test" investment brings a windfall of cash. You can guess what happens next. Good judgment, if not already missing, is obscured by good old-fashioned greed and the mark insists on entrusting a bundle of Benjamin Franklins to the conman, who then disappears with said bundle. Now, most of us are not naïve enough to fall for such a stunt; most of us know that magicians only seem to make doves fly out of silk scarves. But if "most" meant "all" then what use would there be for leisurely sports such as eye-rolling and pointing and laughing at a neighbor? The mark does his best to keep the whole thing quiet, even during the futile "he'll be back" phase. But he can do nothing but hope. And wait. And sweat. And develop a nervous tic while he waits some more. He'll desperately try to make contact, but it's no use. Hope turns to confusion, confusion to anxiety, and anxiety to shock when bleak reality returns like a baseball bat to the forehead.

It's an old trick. The first use of the term "confidence man" dates from 1847, and the elements of the operation then are essentially unchanged now: See fool and his money. See shifty-eyed figure approach with charm and promises. See fool go one way and money another.

It is not clear how elaborate the scheme was that allegedly roped in Floyd Mayweather Jr., but it is becoming obvious that he lost *millions*.

Rumor has it that flim-flammed Floyd fled not to the police, but to the nefarious Don King's office. Too embarrassed to even alert advisor Leonard Ellerbe and manager Al Haymon, Floyd damn near signed a multi-fight deal to make quick money the easy way. King, after all, is generous with signing bonuses. Haymon rushed in with a cool head, prevailed upon his impulsive charge, and took the pen away.

You can decide for yourself whether the story above has the ring of truth or not. If you happen to believe it, it can provide a credible context to recent spectacles. Perhaps you've noticed how amplified the histrionics of the Mayweather tribe have been lately and how preoccupied the press has been with what look like sideshows put on to distract from the real main event.

And the main event ain't pretty.

Mayweather grossed $50 million in 2007. The IRS filed a lien of $6.17 million in unpaid taxes against him last October. Ellerbe denied it, but it's a matter of public record. Keith Kizer, Executive Director of the Nevada State Athletic Commission, told David Mayo of the *Grand Rapid Press* yesterday that a deal had been finalized between Mayweather and the IRS for Mayweather to pay the IRS $5 million. Check the math. Why was Floyd unable to pay a relatively paltry 6.17 million that he owed the IRS after he made more than eight times that amount the previous year?

Here's one answer: that swindler cleaned Mayweather out and left him no choice but to come out of retirement. His lifestyle depended on it.

So the next time he waves those hundred-dollar bills at the cameras, take a good look at whose face is on those bills and note the bemused expression. It says it all.

September 17, 2009

Deconstructing Manny

Manny Pacquiao: *I'm just [an] ordinary fighter.*
Freddie Roach (interrupting): *You're not ordinary.*
Manny Pacquiao: *Sorry about that, master.*

"He finds gaps," said Emanuel Steward after Manny Pacquiao stopped Miguel Cotto in the twelfth round. Those three words mirror the words of a far older, far more legendary war tactician: Sun Tzu. "Strike at their gaps," *The Art of War* asserted two thousand years ago. "Attack when they are lax, don't let the enemy figure out how to prepare." The second knockdown of Cotto illustrated this theory. Cotto, a conventional boxer-puncher, was hit on the chin in the fourth round by an uppercut from the left side that went inside and underneath his guard. Pacquiao found a gap, capitalized on the momentary carelessness of an onrushing opponent, and spent the rest of the fight exploding every solution Cotto thought he had.

"When you are going to attack nearby make it look as if you are going to go a long way," Sun Tzu said. "When you are going to attack far away, make it look as if you are going just a short distance." Pacquiao seems to be moving out when he's coming in and coming in when he's moving out. He exploits expectations with illusions. He "draws them in" and then "takes them by confusion." Trainer Freddie Roach, himself an ex-fighter, agrees that Pacquiao is a puzzle. Pacquiao continues punching when his opponent expects a pause, his angles are bizarre, and he is often not where he is expected to be after a combination. Due to such unorthodoxies, this southpaw is a master of destroying the timing and rhythm of a conventional fighter. He is similar to Joe Calzaghe in that regard. Mikkel Kessler said that Calzaghe "ruins your boxing." Pacquiao does worse than that. Calzaghe spills ink all over your blueprint; Pacquiao ruins your blueprint, but then adds injury to insult by smashing the drafting table over your head.

There's Something About Manny

Pacquiao has athletic gifts that translate well in the ring: disruptive rhythm, timing, and speed all backed up by punching power that belies his featherweight frame. As if this weren't enough, his whiskers safely absorbed the shock of Cotto's left hooks. He was never hurt, which raises eyebrows. Manny, we must remember, was exchanging punches in a division forty pounds north of the one he began in. And he reveled in it, he invited it, even snarling at times and standing disdainfully in the final stanzas to challenge the manhood of the retreating Puerto Rican. Roberto Duran, now fifty-eight, was at ringside. Was he reliving the night he defeated another welterweight who thought he could outfight a smaller man? Duran's coal-black eyes were transfixed as Pacquiao's hair flew with the force of his blows and a smile, once sinister, betrayed his lips.

Despite the glory heaped on him by a celebrity-starved public and an island nation eager for eminence, Pacquiao is not the flawless fighter Duran was when he handed Sugar Ray Leonard his first defeat. Pacquiao's humanity can be sensed if not seen in his nervousness toward the beginning of a bout. It takes him a round or two to find his rhythm and gauge his distance and timing. Before that happens he is prone to reach in, go off balance in range, and leave windows open for counters. After that happens, his opponent, any opponent, is in peril.

He can be controlled, particularly by welterweights, but it will take a trainer and a fighter who are willing to give up conventional strategies and think outside the box. Convention is broken down by revolution, and Manny Pacquiao fights like a revolution.

Alas, even the trainer who recognizes the need for a counter-revolutionary strategy is faced with another problem —the trainer in the opposite corner.

Freddie Roach has Parkinson's disease, which has burdened him with tremors, slurring, and odd pauses during conversations. Its symptoms can be as disconcerting to conventional conversationalists as Manny Pacquiao's style is to conventional fighters; but his disability also gives him an aura of alien brilliance like Stephen Hawking. It has had no effect on his knack for strategy.

Roach did well not to tamper with Pacquiao's unorthodoxy. He streamlined it and added balance, deliberate feints, angles, defense, and a two-fisted attack. Like Floyd Mayweather Jr., Manny Pacquiao has a foundation in fundamentals. Unlike Mayweather, Pacquiao's lessons occurred later in his career, while Floyd's were drilled into him as a small child. Also unlike Mayweather who claims to disdain strategy, Manny enters the ring with a master plan or three. Sun Tzu emphasized this: "Victorious warriors win first and then go to war." Roach spends hours and days and weeks and months in study. He deconstructs his opponent and finds patterns —"habits" as he calls them, to exploit. Then he teaches Manny to "see it as [he] sees it."

At times, the eyes of Freddie Roach seem to focus on a higher plane inaccessible to anyone else. Perhaps he communes with the ghost of Eddie Futch. Futch was his mentor, and is among the greatest trainers of the last century. Freddie Roach learned at his knee; Manny Pacquiao at Freddie's.

Pacquiao is the most popular boxer in the world today. He was catapulted into stardom after he defeated Oscar De La Hoya and then Ricky Hatton. Serious boxing fans know the truth. De La Hoya and Hatton were simply two candles on a cake already baked between 2003 and 2008 by great Mexicans from the lower weight divisions. Marco Antonio Barrera, Erik Morales, and Juan Manuel Marquez tried him much like Murderers' Row tried Archie Moore in the 1940s and Philadelphia did Marvelous Marvin Hagler in the 1970s.

Hail Manny, Full of Grace

Boxing is a character sport first and a skills sport second. Manny's character was formed in a background that is ideal for a fighter, a background set in the kind of third-world poverty that Americans have not known for seventy years. It is a background that spawns fighters in back alleys amid broken bottles and broken dreams. Manny ran away from home at fourteen to spare his mother one more mouth to feed, exchanging real poverty for worse poverty in an act of sacrifice. This fighter has not only suffered, he also understood and embraced self-denial in early adolescence.

The toughest sport in the world is easy for someone like him. Pacquiao has something to fight for as only a poor man can —for self, for family, for country. He has the discipline to do it and he has the perspective to transcend it. The sweet science is meaningful to him. His participation in it is an expression of love and loyalty, of self-actualization. So he approaches the ring with *joy*.

And that isn't all.

Manny believes that the hand of God Almighty is on his shoulder. Cynical secularism may scoff at such ancient notions, but irreverence is irrelevant here. Manny believes this —utterly, and it gives him an edge in that he is completely self-possessed and palpably unconcerned with the risks of the ring. He goes not only willingly, but happily. Throughout history, like-minded people strode confidently into lions' dens, climbed into kamikaze cockpits, blew themselves up at marketplaces, sang while burning at a stake, and volunteered to die first at Nazi death camps to spare strangers. Pacquiao's religiosity is that kind of powerful. It is a major reason why he smiles and waves on his way into battle. Boxing fans take note: his frame of mind was shared by Sugar Ray Robinson and Muhammad Ali.

Emanuel Steward's assertion that Pacquiao, now 50-3-2, belongs "up there" with Ali and Robinson was half wrong. When Robinson was thirty, he was defeated once in one hundred thirty-one bouts and went on to finish his career with the scalps of a dozen world champions hanging from his belt. Manny isn't near that. He is a typhoon blowing over structures less sturdy than those built in the golden era of boxing. But remember, he isn't finished yet.

Like the legends before him, Manny Pacquiao sees himself as a man of destiny; a patriot fighting for a flag, a Christian smiling at lions.

Such men are rarely taken down by anything except time and hubris. They are larger than their foes even when they are not.

Such men are larger than themselves.

November 17, 2009

Shane

Nazeem Richardson believes that Shane Mosley is a problem. "Shane will fight anybody," he said, "and that's not good business. You could convince Shane to fight one of them Klitschkos." He's "just a gladiator," said Richardson.

Gladiators didn't pack heat. Shane does, and when it comes to shooting straight and fast, he's mighty good. He's a gunfighter.

Gunfighters had codes. The Old West needed order even in the absence of lawmen, and these codes were unwritten but understood. They were standards for living when living wasn't for long. "Never wake another man by shaking or touching him," said one of them, "as he might wake suddenly and shoot you dead." "Always drink your whiskey with your gun hand, to show your friendly intentions," went another. Chivalry was upheld: "Cuss all you want, but only around men, horses, and cows." Shane has a few more additions, never written. The trajectory of his career suggests that "duck no one" is the first of them.

Eight years ago this gunfighter got a spur caught on a viper. The late Vernon Forrest fought like a reincarnation of "The Cincinnati Cobra" Ezzard Charles and as a result, ophidiophobia spread through the upper ranks of welterweights. Shane faced Forrest when Oscar De La Hoya, Tito Trinidad, and Ike Quartey wouldn't. Forrest beat him during the 1992 Olympic Trials and when they turned professional he beat him again on a winter's night in 2002, knocking him down twice as he did. Six months later, Shane lost the rematch. Vernon considered him an equal despite these victories.

Six years ago, the gunfighter's punches bounced off of Winky Wright's arms and elbows like popcorn off a movie screen. Wright was, like Forrest, avoided for years. Shane fought him just to prove that he would. He lost. Eleven months later, he fought him again and lost again, by a hairsbreadth. "A lot of fighters ran from me," an appreciative Wright told the press. "Shane was the only one who would fight me."

"This is what fights are about. This is what the boxing world needs," Shane said. "It isn't the money."

It is now.

Floyd "Money" Mayweather is undefeated; but then, so were gunfighters who shot at cans on stumps in a yard. While his talent is undeniable, Floyd has been spending more time shaking his fist at his legions of critics than he has at serious challengers. That zero on his record is more jealously guarded than Sutter's Mill. It sparkles gold in his eyes and he wants it to sparkle in yours, though to his critics the value of that zero is clear. Lest we forget, Shane himself was 38-0 before he accepted the challenge of Vernon Forrest; and he could have matched and surpassed Mayweather's 40-0 years ago had he too taken the primrose path. But he didn't. He has five losses on his record. In a clear head on a clear day, these losses look less like blemishes and more like rebukes of Mayweather.

It doesn't end there. The contrast between Mayweather and other elites in the class over the past few years is stark. Mosley, Miguel Cotto, and Antonio Margarito have all faced each other. Mayweather has been the odd man out. Since his welterweight campaign began in 2005, Mayweather has had six fights. He knocked Sharmba Mitchell down twice en route to a sixth round stoppage, and hoped fans forgot the previous year when Kostya Tszyu knocked Mitchell down twice as much and stopped him twice as fast. Mayweather then faced Zab Judah who had lost to Carlos Baldomir only three months earlier. The plodding Baldomir, whose previous two fights were with two Mayweather conquests, was next. It was what everyone already knew it would be —a clinic. After deflating the ego of a rusty De La Hoya, he answered the challenge of junior welterweight Ricky Hatton, with the contractual condition that they meet at welterweight.

The last time Mayweather was in the ring, he faced a natural featherweight. The contract stipulated that they meet at one hundred forty-four pounds. Floyd added insubordination to insult. He weighed in at one hundred forty-six and paid a $600,000 fine to Juan Manuel Marquez for the advantage. Six months later another natural featherweight from the other side of the world was eating five times a day to keep weight on to fight a welterweight avoided by Mayweather.

On January 3, the expectation that Mayweather would meet Manny Pacquiao disappeared into the horizon as promoter Bob Arum declared the fight "dead." The proxy fight between the two camps continued on a global scale. Shooting began on the internet, in what's left of the dailies, on sports programs, and both sides got personal. The disappointment crossed continents. UFC president Dana White had a shovel in his hand as boxing assumed its usual position of a dead horse.

And then Shane rode in, on a white horse.

Like the stray gunfighter of the same name in Jack Schaefer's novel, "he came steadily on straight through the town without slackening the pace" and moved "steadily on our side." On *our* side. "I don't need the money." Shane has repeatedly said. "I want to fight the biggest fights for the fans, the legacy fights."

Larger forces had a hand in shifting circumstances. A lesser bout against Andre Berto was canceled in the aftermath of an earthquake, and Shane, though gracious, was left among tumbleweeds. When Pacquiao signed to face Joshua Clottey, Floyd was left scanning the field. Shane had boldly challenged him in the ring after he defeated Marquez and he was under pressure to come to terms. It seemed that the ever-elusive Floyd was finally cornered.

"He was forced into it," said Jack Mosley.

The elder Mosley told me that his son has been ready and willing to fight Floyd for at least ten years and that he and Shane have long since deconstructed the Mayweather style. In fact, "he's been beating Floyd up every week for years already," Mosley said, "so unless Floyd does something different, he's going to get beat up again," this time literally. What's more, Mosley believes that Floyd has not improved but devolved. Due to injuries and perhaps even fear, he is not the fighter he was at junior lightweight or lightweight.

How difficult will Floyd be for Shane? Jack scoffs at the question. "I don't think it is going to be a hard fight for Shane," he says. "Unless Floyd decides to run like Bugs Bunny." Forget about Shane's loss to Cotto. Mosley insists that scar tissue in Shane's nose blocked over 40% of his oxygen intake during that fight. It was surgically corrected before the Margarito fight and we all saw the difference. As a result, Shane's conditioning is better now than it has been for years, and Mosley promises that his son is prepared to give Floyd "a whole lot to think about."

Years ago, Shane extended his glove to hungry, avoided fighters. Shane, now thirty-eight, has been avoided himself. The courtesy he gave others is now being returned, albeit from an unlikely source. Shane has an opportunity to prove once and for all that he is the best, if not the fastest, gun in the wild welterweight division. Floyd seeks the same and will stand opposite him in more ways than one. Floyd, who claims that Shane had once refused to fight him because of a "toothache"; Floyd, whom Shane called a lowdown "liar" for even questioning his willingness to fight anybody.

Floyd has been knocking over wagons instead of trains but wants you to believe he's Jesse James. Criticism of his record is valid though it doesn't mean he isn't right. Floyd Mayweather Jr. *is* Jesse James. We've seen his brilliance. Jack Mosley says Floyd has diminished from whatever he was ten years ago, though Mosley may well be wrong. All of his critics may be wrong. Perhaps the true height of Floyd's brilliance is still unknown precisely because he has not been tested. Perhaps his best is yet to be seen.

We'll see it soon because he'll need it.

The mountain resort at Big Bear Lake in California has an elevation near nine thousand feet. The air is thin at that altitude and the scenery is breathtaking. In the solitude of a training camp, where a man's mind narrows to a fine edge and his mission takes on the kaleidoscope colors of a defining moment, an aging gunfighter is polishing his guns.

May 1 at the MGM Grand in Las Vegas is high noon.

April 5, 2010

Floyd

Fortune favors the brave.
—Virgil

Henny Youngman, "The King of the One-Liners," also happened to be a serious boxing fan. He's cracked his last joke, though the laughs roll on. As the Mayweather–Mosley drama recedes into history, one can almost see the comic standing at a celestial microphone: *A gunfighter walks into a bank . . .*

Now, this proverbial bank is celebrated for its high tech security; in fact, no man with guns has ever walked out of it with anything more than a red face and empty hands. But this gunfighter is touted as someone special, someone known for his experience in knocking over other establishments. He manages to dent the vault and it gives a little, at one point even buckling under the weight of a blast, but then something remarkable happens —*the bank shoots back.*

Indeed, it was the offense, not the defense, of Floyd "Money" Mayweather that disarmed Shane Mosley. Forget the rest of the explanations. There is only one reason Shane did not capitalize on the positive proof that he could hurt Floyd: he got convinced that Floyd could hurt him.

It was assumed that Shane was the puncher here, and it was taken for granted that he would be the bigger and stronger man. In the second round, Shane financed that notion with thirteen power punches, two of which almost blew up the bank. But the bank survived and the assumptions blew up as the world watched Floyd bully Shane the rest of the night. It was almost like watching Alan

Greenspan loosen his tie and execute a clean and jerk.

Shane landed only one power punch in the third round and none in the fourth. Floyd not only threw more total punches than Shane, but doubled, tripled, and quadrupled Shane's connect rate in rounds three through twelve. The gunfighter was gun-shy. What happened? A well-conditioned veteran is not gun-shy unless he is concerned about being hit and he would not be concerned about being hit unless the offending shots have power to hurt him. At the post-fight press conference, Nazeem Richardson was asked what adjustment Floyd made in the third round after being on the brink of a knockout loss in the second. Nazeem, who had accurately predicted that a dragon would rise up out of Floyd in this fight, said "that fireball hit us."

For his part, Floyd casually remarked that he could have been the first man to stop Shane had he so pleased. No one laughed. There was no trace of the alleged injuries, the pot shots, the pay-per-view performances that were as exciting as watching a boy with a stick chase a leaf in the wind. Floyd's critics are silenced. Even boxing's version of the GOP, those 'Grizzled Old Purists', must concede that Floyd Mayweather Jr. is a complete fighter. They can gnash their teeth on stogies and growl at his measly forty-one fight record, but the fair-minded among them know great when they see it. And Floyd is great.

How great?

The answer is a paradox in two parts.

Floyd Mayweather Jr. Is Not As Great As He Claims

Leonard Ellerbe is Floyd's advisor. He should position himself strategically at his interviews and stand at the ready. When Floyd begins to declare his superiority to Sugar Ray Robinson, Ellerbe should pull the plug on the microphone or pop him with a tack.

The numbers don't lie. Robinson had already faced and defeated three Hall of Famers a total of five times when he reached 40-0. He was twenty-one years old. At no less than a dozen years older,

Mayweather has forty wins and one gift. When Robinson was thirty-three years old, he had been in the professional ring over three times as often as Floyd and had by then defeated eight Hall of Famers seventeen times. His record was 131-3-2 with eighty-six knockouts. Read it again and watch Floyd shrink. In his determination to convince the world of his primacy, Floyd would do well to avoid comparisons between himself and the fistic deities of the past. The reason is simple: even the best of bronze looks dull next to polished gold.

If Ellerbe lacks the nerve to straighten him out, then self-proclaimed boxing historian Uncle Roger should take his nephew aside for some honest talk.

Floyd Mayweather Jr. Is Greater Than He Believes

After nearly five years of campaigning in the welterweight division, Floyd has finally accomplished what another Sugar did almost thirty years ago: he defeated a particularly dangerous rival.

There are interesting parallels between the personalities of Ray Leonard and Floyd Mayweather Jr. Both double as savvy, image-conscious celebrities who have a strain of what seems to be insecurity. It is detectable if you look closely.

Neither has been above seeking advantages before a fight. In the rematch against Roberto Duran, Leonard admitted that he intentionally lured Duran back into the ring only five months after their first bout because he knew Duran's gluttony would affect his conditioning. Leonard tried to ignore Thomas Hearns until public pressure reached fever pitch and forced him to the table. He also managed to get several concessions against Marvin Hagler, including a larger ring, bigger gloves, and fewer rounds. Floyd's choices of opponents over the past three years suggest a similar pattern. These patterns suggest insecurity.

Neither have had many fights. Boxing is a means to an end for them, not an end in and of itself. What Leonard craved was the limelight. Impressive wins as a young Olympian and professional made him a superstar but he was either retiring or ready to retire after a tough bout or a big win. For Floyd, those C-notes he flashes are only emblems of the grandiose self-image he has built, and his glory is rooted in his undefeated record. Whether he responds to critics of his record with fallacious argument or acknowledges their right to an opinion is beside the point. The details really don't matter to him; the address for Floyd National Bank is just as good on Easy Street as it would be on Concussion Ave or Pain Lane.

He just cleaned the clock of an elite welterweight; but what is being suggested here is that had he, in the silence of his solitude and in his heart of hearts, truly believed in himself, he'd have already cleaned out the whole division.

Floyd is not as great as he claims, but he is greater than he believes. That statement is not slinging mud so much as pointing to the stars. Important decisions must be made by this special athlete. He should feel encouraged, now more than ever, to seek high-risk bouts. The returns are of the forever type. If he chooses instead to sit on a single laurel and insist, as he has lately, that "all roads lead to Floyd," then his legacy will be about as solvent as a Greek bank.

May 23, 2010

The Broken Man

When the Japanese mend broken objects, they aggrandize the damage by filling the cracks with gold.
—Barbara Bloom

Sonny Liston was a broken man when he became the heavyweight champion of the world. The product of a disturbing past, he looked out from behind a mask and saw a hostile world aligned against him. Where an adolescent with a healthy self-image develops morale, Liston developed a different brand of motivation. It looked like revenge. If a secondhand confession by one of his seconds is true, he was also a cheat. That's no surprise; broken men are often desperate men, and desperate men are often amoral.

Antonio Margarito is not far from the dark place where Liston was.

Manny Pacquiao, by contrast, is lighthearted. He is much more than that. The transcendental fighter we saw last year has transformed himself into a transcendental figure on the world stage. In June, I sat in the Grand Ballroom of the Roosevelt Hotel in Manhattan during the Boxing Writers Association of America's Awards Dinner and watched him walk to a podium above a squall of flashing bulbs. His poise was perfect as he delivered a well-crafted speech from memory. Most fighters are pugnacious when a microphone is stuck in their grill. This one was presidential. Congressman Emmanuel Dapidran Pacquiao doesn't need boxing anymore. He has found a new and exciting venue to raise not only the spirits of his countrymen, but their quality of life.

As Manny looks up with plans to soar, his latest Mexican opponent looks down and broods. And he's a big one. Joshua Clottey should have proved too strong for Manny, but instead proved unable to overcome an innate aversion to risk that traveled the short distance between his psyche and his style. He could not mount a sustained attack.

Margarito will have no such inhibitions.

Remember the original Hands of Stone. Every one of Duran's accomplishments after 1980 was a desperate telegram from a fallen hero fighting for his very name, for redemption. Margarito seeks the same. He believes he has what all of us sinners wish we had —a once-in-a-lifetime opportunity to cancel out his disgrace in one night. This by itself makes him dangerous.

Victory is possible if he proves durable enough to absorb a Pacquiao blast and avoid the exclamations coming after it. If Margarito is able to force the smaller man backwards, he may be able to do what Clottey failed to try to do; and that is physically dominate the best fighter on the planet.

It is possible, though not likely.

Manny is a complex counter-puncher who fights in three dimensions; Margarito, a predictable pressure fighter who fights in one. In defying his strength and conditioning coach's recommendation to gain more weight, Manny is affirming an old school tenet: be natural. Margarito will enter the ring a middleweight, but he is as naturally slow as Manny is naturally fast. He can and will be nailed by counters. Manny may not have the muscle mass to handle Margarito in the clinches or even fight him for long in the trenches, but neither is part of the Roach strategy. That strategy complements a confusing style energized by speed and precision. Manny zeroes in on nerve centers —the short left landed on the right side of David Diaz's jaw, the left hook on the right side of Ricky Hatton's jaw, the right to Miguel Cotto's left temple and right uppercut to the point of his chin—and fires his punches within the blink of an eye. They don't land so much as detonate on those nerve centers.

On Saturday night, Margarito's nerve centers will be as easy to find as they would be on any other Saturday night. He will climb four stairs anyway, this broken man, and millions will watch him try to fill his cracks with gold.

November 12, 2010

Onward, Christian Soldier

Be merciful, just as your Father is merciful.
—Luke 6:36

After the bout between Manny Pacquiao and Antonio Margarito was signed in July, trainer Freddie Roach holed up for hours to study the fight films of Margarito. As he watched and analyzed his style, he began to compare performances. Soon suspicions mounted. He concluded that Margarito's gloves were loaded against two opponents —Kermit Cintron and Miguel Cotto. "You look at those guys after the fight," Roach said. "It looked like a truck hit them."

A few of his own fighters had sparred with Margarito during that time and what they told him connected the dots of his theory. Rashad Holloway, one of those fighters, considered suing Margarito. He suffered a broken eye socket while sparring Margarito about two years ago. "I don't think he's really recovered from that yet," said Roach. Had it been his decision, Margarito would have been suspended from boxing for life after he was caught cheating in January 2009. Instead, Roach gave a bitter nudge to karma: "I hope Manny Pacquiao kicks his a** for all those people [he hurt] out there."

Margarito was taken by ambulance to the hospital early Sunday morning. The facial injuries he suffered included a broken nose, cuts and severe swelling around the eyes, and a broken orbital bone: that is, a broken eye socket. He spent the night under the care of physicians. He remains there as of this writing.

The fight didn't begin badly for the bigger man. After the third round, Margarito returned to his corner and said "he can't hurt me."

115

Then the bell rang for the fourth and within moments it became painfully clear that Pacquiao, notwithstanding dramatic size and strength disadvantages, could indeed hurt him. Margarito emerged from an exchange with a damaged right eye. Two minutes later he emerged from the round with a new CompuBox record: he had never before been punched more times in one round. His hubris, before and during the fight, seemed to have a price in blood. A crowd of forty-one thousand watched a beating that would have won the approval of any subscriber to the Law of Retaliation.

In nearly every minute of the next six rounds, Margarito was taken apart by an offensive machine that some might have mistaken for the Hammer of Justice. By the end of the tenth round, Margarito's face was bludgeoned into disfigurement. The roars of Cowboys Stadium were like echoes across nineteen centuries, blending with the roars of the Flavian Amphitheater in anticipation of a finale most brutal. The referee stopped the action a few times to ensure that Margarito could see out of his right eye but did not stop the slaughter. When it became clear that his corner would not intervene either, only one figure was left to stand between Margarito and the shadow of death, and it was the most unlikely one.

Sugar Ray Robinson was the greatest fighter that anyone alive has ever seen. In 1947, his fists killed Jimmy Doyle in a title bout. Robinson was horrified. The coroner asked if he "noticed that Doyle was in trouble at any time." Robinson's answer was the answer of any man who fights for a living: "—Getting him in trouble is my business."

Manny Pacquiao answered the same question not as a fighter but as a Christian. He knew that Margarito was no longer a threat to anyone but himself, and sensed that he was in mortal danger. In the eleventh round he stopped punching and pleaded with the referee. "Look at his eyes, look at his cuts," Manny told him and then us, "I did not want to damage him permanently. That is not what boxing is about." Despite the exhortation of the crowd and the glory that would come with a late-round knockout of the most menacing fighter he ever faced, he began punching less and pulling his punches. Manny, in other words, carried Margarito.

"I feel pity to him," said the greatest fighter of this generation. *I feel pity to him.*

Manny was once destitute on the streets of Manila. His mythical fists were once miserable hands opened for alms. He remembers when he himself was on the brink of collapse and he remembers who carried him through it.

He felt pity for Margarito because he knows Margarito is himself.

Two thousand years ago, someone special taught his misfit band of followers about the Golden Rule and faith and power and the power of faith. He told them that the power of faith can move mountains. In overcoming the biggest challenger of his career, Manny proved him right yet again; and in resisting the vengeful urges of Roach, he returned a favor owed. His faith moved a mountain called Margarito. Margarito, whose blood atonement was canceled out; Margarito, who was carried in the last round almost as gently as a good shepherd would carry an injured lamb —or a broken man.

November 15, 2010

Reflections in the Red-Light District

One loses force when one pities.
—Friedrich Nietzsche, THE ANTI-CHRIST [1895]

"**T**his is getting stranger and stranger," said Ferdie Pacheco after Mike Tyson took a bite out of Evander Holyfield's ear. "We're getting to see strange things happen in boxing."

Seven hundred and forty-three Saturday nights later, we watched young Victor Ortiz billy-goat Floyd Mayweather Jr. after backing him up against the ropes. We watched him apologize to Mayweather with a kiss after referee Joe Cortez stopped the action to escort him around the ring for a point deduction. We wondered why Cortez called "time-in" and then averted his attention from the action. We winced when Ortiz stepped toward Mayweather to apologize yet again and witnessed Mayweather return the clumsy embrace. Suddenly, lightning in the form of a left hook and right hand obliterated the familiar rhythm of the scene. Ortiz had only begun to move casually out of the embrace with his gloves dangling at his sides. He neither saw nor expected the punch that knocked him out. Neither did we.

Larry Merchant called it a legal sucker punch, which is about right. Many fans and internet pundits point to the flagrant foul committed against Mayweather and applaud his delayed ruthlessness. "This isn't a gentleman's sport," Mayweather says. "It's a hurtin' game!" A boxing proverb ("protect yourself at all times") has

119

become a regular chant.

They're not wrong, though that's not the end of it.

There's something else that few are acknowledging, something older and wiser that doesn't shout or gloat or drink from the skulls of the vanquished. It whispers underneath the din. The depleting ranks of an older generation called it the Golden Rule: "do unto others as you would have them do unto you." How quaint. They had a children's fable that went along with it, promising judgment on how well they upheld it. It isn't something we encounter much anymore; just another fraying relic to pitch on the growing heap of a dead morality. Perhaps it is recyclable. Shall we update it with the civic poison of the cynic? *Do unto others as they would do unto you —only do it first.*

Is that what it's all about?

Floyd thinks so, and he's got a pattern of behaviors to prove it. This isn't the first time he exploited a situation to gain an advantage. Two years ago he signed to fight Juan Manuel Marquez, a natural featherweight. The contracted weight for the fight was one hundred forty-four pounds, with fines to be paid in the amount of $300,000 per pound over that weight. Marquez came in two pounds less than the limit. And Mayweather? He shrugged his shoulders, weighed in two pounds more than the weight limit, and paid the $600,000 fine with a smirk. The pundits grumbled at this. Here was a supreme stylist who snatched an additional weight advantage that he didn't even need; here was the in-your-face star of 24/7, with just enough shame to disallow HBO from weighing him before the fight, so no one would know how much of a weight advantage he actually had.

Mayweather did not breach that agreement any more than he breached the rules last Saturday, what he did was sneer at it. That was why the pundits grumbled; an athlete who sneers at an agreement is an athlete who sneers at sportsmanship.

"When you fight for a living," said the infamously unsportsmanlike Fritzie Zivic, "if you're smart you fight with every trick you know."

Fritzie boasted nine zillion of them. He butted his opponents like Ortiz, mauled them, stomped on their feet, used his elbow like Mayweather, and choked his opponents whenever he could. *"Do unto others as they would do unto you —only do it first."* He had nothing but disdain for fighters who fought by the book. According to Zivic virtue, "the book is something you could clout a guy with if you had it ready." In his retirement he would reflect fondly on his fistic memories, among them a gem from 1943, a one-rounder against Vinnie Vines at Madison Square Garden:

> *"In the first round we got tangled up in a clinch and when he stepped out of the clinch he extended his gloves to me. I reached out and hit him a right hand on the chin. Knocked him out."*

It could've been last week. *The Associated Press* reported that Vines "went down with a thump. He tried to get up at the count of nine but fell back, starry eyed." Afterward, Fritzie dismissed his opponent as easily as he dismissed conventional ideas of fair play. "There was nothing to it," he said in the dressing room. "I can keep on fighting until I'm 50 if I meet boys like him."

"That's boxing," said Fritzie.

Is it?

Three years after the Vines fight, Fritzie's manager asked him if he wanted to take a trip to Memphis to fight one Russell Wilhite for an easy payday. The manager asked him if he was in shape. "I don't have to be in shape," said Fritzie. "Any fighter with a name like that cannot fight." Just the same, he brought a pair of gloves that weighed about five ounces, with three of those ounces at the wrists. Why huff and puff through all those rounds when you can get him out of there and go home early? In the dressing room, he got a look at his opponent. Wilhite was still in high school and Fritzie thought he looked like a choir boy. But then something dark whispered inside his balding head, "choir boys have good lungs," it said, "and those light gloves might not be enough of an edge." So he loaded his hands with electrical tape.

And why not? Once time-honored rules of decency are shaken off, the rest is easy. A world-class fighter becomes something less than world class and sometimes something less than a man. The modern cynic couldn't care less. He has declared himself immune to judgment and scoffs at any appeal to a dead morality. He exercises his fundamental right to do as he pleases and he has the whole rotten, stinking world to stick it to. "Nice fellows in boxing get it in the neck," went one of Zivic's zingers. Another one could be engraved on the Mayweather family crest: "The winners make the money, the losers make the excuses."

Fritzie would tell you lots of things. After his career ended, he was still at it, telling lots of things to lots of people as a car salesman. Floyd Mayweather Jr. tells you lots of things too. He smirks and shrugs his shoulders and hasn't the faintest feeling of regret for what he did, least of all for hurling obscenities at an eighty-year-old commentator. "You ain't sh*t!" he said to Larry Merchant after Merchant had the gall to question his sportsmanship. Mayweather now insists that Merchant needs to be fired. "Out with the old and in with the new," he told the world as his fair-weather friends cheered him on. "Only the strong survive." Frederick Nietzsche cheered with them.

Something else went unrecognized and ignored. Something older than Merchant and wiser than Nietzsche that doesn't shout or gloat or drink from the skulls of the vanquished. If you listen with your heart you might hear it, even here in the red-light district of sports, whispering its golden truth above the din.

September 23, 2011

Small Consolation for Plant-Eaters

In the early 1990s, I was one of a ragtag band of boxers who trained at the Boston YMCA on Huntington Avenue. Sparring matches were held on Monday, Wednesday, and Friday evenings and were closely monitored by licensed trainers. After hours, things got nasty. The licensed trainers drifted out and renegade trainers drifted in and held unauthorized bouts where weight classes didn't matter and headgear was frowned upon. Bloodstains splattered the walls around the ring. There were bloodstains on the *ceiling*.

One night I stood across from an opponent who had a sculpted torso like Marvin Hagler, or, come to think of it, Tim Bradley. You could grate Parmigiano-Reggiano on his abs. When the bell rang, I proceeded with caution. He was quick, and stepped in to land a flush right hand. I should have seen stars. But I didn't. I threw a lazy jab on purpose to test his power again on my terms. He did as expected and countered with another right. I turned my head with it, riding it out to gauge its force. For a fighter, especially one who routinely fought for his life in underground smokers, what I learned in that first round was a great relief. He hit about as hard as Aunt Madge.

Privately after the bout, I asked him if he was a vegetarian. The question surprised him and he answered that he was. "Go and get yourself a steak," I said. "Plant-eaters don't beat carnivores." He offered what I'm sure was an impressive oration about healthy protein alternatives like tofu and soybeans though I didn't much know what he was talking about and my parting remark told him I didn't much care: *"Tofu ain't flesh."*

Untold numbers in the holistic health field believe that human beings are natural herbivores; that our hands are designed for berry-picking, not holding down prey and that our so-called canines are too small and flat to tear out flesh. What's more, they say that our digestive systems have not yet adapted to meat and cite studies connecting obesity, heart disease, and other health risks to the neighborhood butcher shop. Under the glaring light of new science, my flip remarks look like medieval superstition. Or do they? Within a few months, my plant-eating opponent became less enlightened: he added red meat to his diet. Already quick-fisted with sound technique, his punching power was soon denting my ribs and we both knew why.

Civilians have every reason to eat tofu and beans in lieu of meat, to build their lifestyles around health consciousness, comfort, and self-preservation. But don't mistake them for fighters. Humanist Dr. Harold Hillman doesn't. He identifies what he calls the "vegetarian conscience" and lists activities that "vegetarian personalities" could be logically expected to vigorously oppose: between "child labor" and "infanticide" sits "boxing." In his defense, I suspect that his ability to appreciate the sweet science is no more advanced than my ability to appreciate the sedentary lifestyle of a soft-bellied academic.

Sugar Ray Robinson's decidedly anti-humanist achievement of knocking out ninety-seven men would horrify Dr. Hillman. His carnivorous habits would have called for smelling salts to revive Dr. Hillman. At a contract-signing luncheon in Chicago before his sixth match against Jake LaMotta in 1951, Robinson asked the waiter for a big glass of beef blood. The waiter was as confused as LaMotta was disturbed. "I'll get you some extra gravy right away," he said. "No, not the gravy," Robinson corrected him. "The actual blood, the blood in the meat before it's cooked." When the glass was set down before him, he turned to LaMotta. "It's what makes a skinny guy like me so strong," he said as he added a pinch of salt and pepper.

"You're outta your mind," said LaMotta.

To the uninitiated, anyone who gets into the ring is "outta his mind." Indeed, if self-preservation and material pursuits are all that matter, then risking one's life for a chance at glory can only be insane.

It's been over ten years since the Boston YMCA on Huntington Avenue ended its boxing program. Odds are four-to-one that the executive director was a vegetarian.

Last night, four-to-one underdog Tim Bradley was given a dubious decision over Manny Pacquiao at the MGM Grand. I predicted a knock out of the most violent sort and though I didn't mention it, part of my reasoning was rooted in the same evidence-based superstition that prompted me to warn my opponent all those years ago: *plant-eaters don't beat carnivores.* Bradley is the picture of health and wellness. His discipline goes beyond that of mere vegetarianism during training camp, he becomes downright vegan and refrains from consuming any animal product. No meat. No fish. No milk. He makes the not-outlandish claim that all that green leafy stuff gives him a surplus of energy. I'm a believer. Had it not been for what hand-wringing academics deplore as a most unfortunate choice of occupations, he'd probably live to be a hundred and ten.

But he sure can't hit.

Despite the fact that Bradley understands how to fight southpaws enough to move to his left, away from their power line, his offense was of the "get off me!" variety. It reminded me of those Animal Planet episodes where a soon-to-be-consumed herbivore flails in a panic just before the beast clamps down on its throat. Pacquiao stalked without fear and shook off left hooks and right hands like a prep cook would wet lettuce.

I watched the bout three times in a vain attempt to see how it was that the judges decided in favor of the Plant-Eater. "I thought Bradley gave Pacquiao a boxing lesson," said Las Vegas judge Duane Ford. "I went in with a clear mind." That's hard to reconcile given that Bradley was outlanded by Pacquiao in ten of twelve rounds. The scattered punches that Bradley did manage to land inflicted no damage and the fact that he landed only nineteen percent of them confirms that they weren't much more than panicky flurries. Panicky flurries constitute neither "clean, effective punching" nor "effective aggression," both of which are a major part of the judging criteria. My scorecard was 117-112 for Pacquiao.

That knockout I predicted was there all night. Had Pacquiao reversed his direction —had he simply gone right instead of left— those left blasts he landed would have ended matters once and for all. He gave Bradley the assist he needed because he wasn't positioning his back foot in front of Bradley's chin in a straight line, in the power line. As it was, Pacquiao and newly-inducted Hall of Fame trainer Freddie Roach neither saw nor made the adjustment. The lion circled the lamb in the wrong direction but proved it was a lion, and the lamb flailed, survived, and took a split decision that defies explanation.

Then again, perhaps none of last night's blunders defy explanation. According to holistic gurus, meat promotes over-acidification of the body and one of the symptoms is "unclear thinking." In that case, someone needs to check the books at Tom Coliccio's Craftsteak at the MGM Grand, where the portions are big and the porterhouse is still breathing.

Four to one says judges Ford and CJ Ross have standing reservations from way back.

June 10, 2012

"¡CANELO!"

The MGM Grand was a madhouse in the hours before Floyd Mayweather Jr.'s bout against Saul "Canelo" Alvarez. The world's most devoted fight fans arrived in torrents —Mexicans, Mexican-Americans, and honorary Mexicans pining for Floyd's defeat. Young males roamed the casino in well-decorated packs and red "Canelo" headbands bobbed in every direction. Some wore capes in answer, I suppose, to their idol's recent appearance in a Superman T-shirt.

One enthusiast paraded back and forth between the lobby and the casino under a red sombrero, wearing oversized green, white, and red boxing gloves and tooting a vuvuzela in three-blast intervals. He did this for hours though no one paid him any mind. They never do in Vegas. It's the only place on earth where a two-headed transvestite in six-inch stilettos could bet on little more than a passing glance —but I'm from Boston, where nonsense is quickly noted and often dealt with. I narrowed my eyes at the vuvuzela-blower; I saw that his face was painted white.

Canelo's red hair and freckles are unusual, though not unheard of, in México. His maternal surname is "Barragán" which sounds Irish, and it's a fact that the Irlandes-Mexicanos have been in the country since the early nineteenth century. It's just as likely that his maternal line goes back to northwestern Spain, a region settled by the Celts during the Iron Age, and it should be noted that a significant percentage of México's population is of European descent. Canelo himself was asked about his ethnicity. "I have no clue," was

127

his answer.

"CANELO! CANELO!" erupted in the MGM Grand Arena whenever his image appeared on the monitors. Mexican fans reminded everyone of just how strong a majority they were on this night. Nothing could silence them, not even the junior welterweight fracas that would crown "Philly Rican" Danny Garcia the true divisional champion according to the *Transnational Boxing Rankings Board*. When the "Star-Spangled Banner" was sung before the main event, they were downright reverent until the balladeer capped off his performance with an unwise shout-out: "Money Team! Let's go!" That got him jeered right out of the joint.

Things calmed down when sixteen thousand seven hundred forty-six souls were serenaded by a beautiful rendition of "México Lindo y Querido" during Canelo's ring walk. It touched the heart of everyone familiar with the song. Carlos Aguirra, a sports writer for Zeta made sure that my heart was touched too when he translated the refrain. *"Lovely, beloved México. If I die away from you, tell them I'm asleep and may they bring me back here."* He reminded me that it was the preferred entrance song of Julio Cesar Chavez, the most celebrated Mexican champion in history.

When Jimmy Lennon Jr. introduced Canelo, I thought the roof would shimmy up like the lid of a steam pot. Chavez was there. He was cheering too.

The fight itself proved anticlimactic. Despite the adoration, undefeated record, physical advantages, and the surprising poise exhibited by the twenty-three-year-old Canelo, he was in over his head. Weeks before the fight, *Esquina* asked me for a prediction. I said that their national hero has serious stamina issues; that he is a stop-and-go fighter with a tendency to fade around the sixth round. This would prove to be a drag on any strategy his corner came up with. Floyd, I said, knew this. He would fight the stronger man on wheels and from the outside to frustrate and wear him out on the way to a unanimous decision or even a late stoppage.

At the opening bell, Canelo moved toward Mayweather —and then took a step backward. It was a message to Mayweather that he would box and conserve his energy. He lost at that moment. Knowledgeable fans murmured, but still their flags were vigorously waved, vuvuzelas were vigorously tooted, and the familiar chants of "Canelo!" and "México!" still raised the roof. Midway through the first round, they began chanting *"Si se puede! Si se puede!"* I asked Aguirra about it. He said it means "yes, we can" and that it has been a staple of Mexican sports culture since Guadalupe won the 1997 Little League World Series. I thought it signaled desperation setting in early, like someone plonked a ball and chain on winged victory.

Canelo's ball and chain, his stamina problems, were dragging down his hope of victory in the sixth round, right on schedule. By the seventh, Floyd was flinching at Canelo, who looked more and more like the schoolyard victim he once was. It wasn't a contest anymore. It was a clinic. Floyd jabbed to elicit an expected reaction, then countered a full second before anyone else would. Canelo's shots breezed past a rolling, pivoting, playful Floyd.

The ear-busting chants had all but ended by the eighth round. Every now and then a lone woman or a dedicated little group would stand up and shout "Canelo! Canelo!" as their neighbors sagged in their seats and lowered their flags.

At the end of the eleventh, some gathered up their things and began leaving, their faces etched in disappointment. The last thing the young hero did in the twelfth round was throw a one-two against a ring general who laughs at simple tactics. By then, silence had set in.

In defeating the *Transnational Boxing Rankings Board's* number one junior middleweight contender, Floyd (who was ranked number two) assumed a throne eight years vacant. He was a gracious winner. "I take my hat off to México," he said during the post-fight interview. "México has produced some great champions throughout the years." Those astute enough to ignore the silly claims of the sanctioning bodies count no less than forty since 1942. Canelo's black eye was only one indication that he has work to do before he claims a throne for himself. "We didn't have answers," he said to his countrymen who were streaming away. "I didn't want to lose. It hurts."

I headed further back in the nosebleed sections to see what I could see in terms of the real story. I saw a drunk teetering up the ramp toward section two hundred twenty-one bellowing "Ca-nel-o! Ca-nel-o!" with his arms raised in mock victory. He was grinning stupidly as the crowd descended from the bleachers and filed past him. A few women looked askance at him; a few men glared. He looked back at them with eyes like egg whites and went at it again—"Ca-nel-o! Ca-nel-o!" I stepped off to one side expecting a thirteenth round of sorts. Luckily for him, everyone's passion was spent. "Bah!" someone said over a shoulder. "I'm a Chicano from East L.A.!"

A few minutes later, I watched two young men turn the corner in silence with eyes on the floor. One of them reached up and flicked off his red headband. His friend looked over and quickly did the same.

One fan wearing the flag of México around his shoulders waxed defiant. "He looks Irish," he said to no one in particular. Then he pulled the beloved flag close to his heart, and walked on.

September 16, 2013

The Historic Fifth Crown

In 1988, Sugar Ray Leonard defeated Donny Lalonde and was handed two world championships for the price of none. HBO's Larry Merchant sniffed at this. After a post-fight studio discussion with Leonard, he turned to us. "You may have noticed I made no reference to Sugar Ray Leonard winning his fourth and fifth world championships. This may be the sincerest form of flattery because the promoters have invented three titles for every two pounds. The fallout is that the word 'champion' means less than the fighter, who is or isn't one."

It's an old complaint, but the problem has become worse; exponentially worse. The sanctioning bodies are actively inventing new championships to increase their ill-gotten gains and thrive on the confusion. "These organizations hand out belts like business cards," sniffed Showtime's Mauro Ranallo last Saturday night. Boxing's appeal has suffered as a result. The U.S. has bad indicators in sports bars where boxing never comes up and on barber shop walls that display no autographed 8x10s that say "keep punching." Last week I was on Boylston Street in Boston looking for a little hope. I reached out to a fellow citizen. "Ten bucks if you can tell me who the middleweight champion of the world is." I held up a sawbuck between two fingers. "Oh man," he said, tapping his chin. I offered a hint. "He's Puerto Rican, bald, and tattooed like a sideshow. Throws left hooks." Silence. Then a faraway look. "... I remember when Hagler was champ," he said.

Mayor Tom Menino didn't. After the Red Sox won the World Series and the Patriots won the Super Bowl in 2004, Menino referred to Boston as "The City of Champions" and the people of Brockton, an economically distressed city twenty-five miles south, came out swinging. They had laid claim to that title long ago, in the name of favorite sons Rocky Marciano and Marvelous Marvin Hagler. One Brockton resident was irate enough to challenge the rotund mayor to a boxing match, in the name of yesterday.

We look behind us, and while that's always advisable in the red-light district, it also makes sense in a sport that builds so directly on the past. Our fighters, hallowed be their names, are not only strong-willed athletes but libraries of accumulated ring knowledge. When those who inspire us the most die, they won't be found moldering under crabgrass in some out-of-the-way cemetery like the rest of us. We recast them into statues, larger than life and forever young, standing guard in their old neighborhoods like Achilles in Corfu.

Some of them are kings.

We look behind us to see, what, if not successions of warring kings?

"We know who the real fighters are," Merchant said at the end of the Leonard-Lalonde broadcast. We no longer know who the real champions are.

It's the boxing historians, the independent specialists, who should have answers. There's squabbling among them to be sure, but they are more relevant now than ever before. They'll tell you Ray Leonard is a three-division king; no more, no less. They'll also tell you only two have conquered four weight divisions, and they happen to be the top two welterweights in the world today.

History, With an Asterisk

In 1937-1938, when Henry Armstrong stormed the featherweight, lightweight, and welterweight divisions inside of ten months, there were only eight recognized divisions. We call them "glamour divisions" and Armstrong held three of their crowns simultaneously.

Only Bob Fitzsimmons matched this achievement (middle-weight, 1891; heavyweight, 1897; light heavyweight, 1903), though it took him nearly thirteen years. No one else has taken more than two of those eight crowns; not even Sugar Ray Robinson, though it was only outside interference that stopped him. In July 1941, he easily defeated the first-rated lightweight in the world only to be left out in the cold when the lightweight king gave the man he defeated a title shot. In June 1952, he made a grab for the light heavyweight crown but was done in by heat prostration in a ring that would reach over a hundred degrees under the lights. "God beat me!" he said afterwards in his dressing room, in his delirium. Think about that. Robinson, a welterweight and middleweight king, would have con-quered four glamour divisions (a forty-pound span) had fate merely cracked a smile.

Fate has been one big smiley-face for Floyd Mayweather Jr. and Manny Pacquiao. Between Armstrong's reign in 1938 and Arm-strong's death in 1988, the number of crowns available jumped from eight to seventeen. The invention and reactivation of in-between and junior divisions, some of which are only four pounds apart, have primrosed the path to the crowns. Mayweather has won the crown in four divisions: jr. lightweight, lightweight, welterweight, and jr. middleweight. Pacquiao has matched him, albeit in four dif-ferent divisions: flyweight, featherweight, jr. lightweight, and jr. wel-terweight.

Now something unprecedented is within their reach; something that outshines the tin belts around it like the Nevada sun outshines dashboard lights in a car going nowhere: the *fifth* crown. If main-stream sports media pick up on it and are clear about what it means, it could spark something of a renaissance. It could return boxing to front-page news.

To lay hands on it, Mayweather must fight jr. welterweight king Danny Garcia at 140 or middleweight king Miguel Cotto at 160. If he is serious about his legacy and stops confusing grandeur with grudges, he will come to terms with Top Rank and challenge Cotto.

The middleweight crown would not only be his fifth, it would enshrine him alongside Armstrong and Fitzsimmons as one of only three glamour-division kings in the record books.

Pacquiao must fight Mayweather at welterweight or jr. middleweight, or stablemate Cotto at middleweight. He therefore has three paths by which he can seize his fifth crown, two of which will see history's three glamour-division kings become a trinity of diversity. The fact that the Filipino's first crown was at flyweight, fifty pounds south of middleweight, would make such an achievement as remarkable as Armstrong's, and that's nothing to sniff at.

Never mind the buzz leaking out of Mayweather's camp about his secret plan "to fight Pacquiao next year"; they're squaring off already. The question is who will face and defeat the right opponent in the right weight class, and do it first. That's front-page news.

Expect *Mayweather vs. Pacquiao Redux* in 2015.

July 21, 2014

The Good Fight

"The fans deserve to have a good fight," said Manny Pacquiao at Friday's weigh-in. Floyd Mayweather Jr. was less congenial. "My frame of mind is to be smart," he said.

The smart fighter defeated the congenial fighter by at least eight rounds on Saturday night.

When Pacquiao was pressed about why he missed eighty-one percent of his punches, he shrugged his shoulders. "If he stays, I can hit him. If he's moving, I can't." When trainer Freddie Roach was asked what he thought of the victorious Mayweather, he smirked and said, "I thought he ran very well."

Mayweather ran from Pacquiao no more than a matador runs from a bull. He teased him with a jab, jutting it out and waving it like a red flag. When Pacquiao began to charge, he stepped back to set a trap. When Pacquiao cornered him, he tied him up or spun off to center-ring. Throughout the match, his left mesmerized an oddly subdued Pacquiao and his right stabbed him with surprising ease, though there would be no *coup de grâce*. It was a master class of athletic efficiency and strategic planning.

Mayweather showed the world what the sweet science looks like.

He was booed at the end of it. Many are still booing him and the sweet science itself at that. "Pay-per-snooze," sneered *USA Today* on Sunday. "A glorified sparring match." *The Atlantic* ran an article entitled "Boxing's Boring Night." *Slate* added an intensifier to its headline "...Very Boring Fight of the Century." ESPN's Skip Bayless scoffed at Mayweather's supposed "preening" and "smoke and mirrors." Drew Magary of *Deadspin* threw rocks from a safe perch, linking the champion's boxing style to his character and condemning both ("Floyd Mayweather Is a Coward").

Pundits spent the last nineteen years sitting around thinking about topics and drinking coffee; Mayweather spent it fighting his way to the top of the most dangerous combat sport in the world. He did it mindfully, because despite his "TBE" boasts and postures, he is acutely aware of the fragility of the human body. He has built a career and a style around that awareness. It isn't cowardice.

Anyone who has spent enough time in a boxing gym has seen firsthand what happens to fighters who shrug off punches and grin like gargoyles instead of moving their heads —what happens after too many "good fights." Perhaps you've seen them too, the graying ones who shuffle into gyms, pitched forward like the brawlers they used to be. They come in alone, always alone, and stand at the periphery staring vacantly. They may ask for a handout or something more. More than money is memory; theirs and yours. Do you remember their ring wars? "That was a good fight," you say, and their eyes meet your eyes, and the "thank you" sounds like boot-crunched leaves.

Mayweather has seen the ghosts in the afternoon, many times.

His critics haven't. They don't see what he's seen. They don't even see *him*. They see Mayweather the obnoxious minstrel on television and want to lay a rose on Joe Louis's grave. They see court records about battered ex-girlfriends and traumatized child witnesses and wonder if any of his fights were worth the price of admission. Some of them look incredulously at modern American culture itself; a culture twisted enough to not only produce but enrich low-lifes like him.

I was among them Sunday morning, until I stepped away from the dueling narratives and took another look, a closer look. It began at the post-fight press conference when Mayweather asked us to remember his and our own humanity. "A lot of people tried to turn this fight into good versus evil. I didn't really care to entertain that. Manny has made mistakes just like I've made mistakes. No one is perfect. Each and every day we both need to grow and become better human beings."

That was sharper than any right he threw all night. And it landed flush.

He spoke for a full thirty-five minutes about his and really every fighter's need to defend himself, about the importance of being calculating on both sides of the ropes, mindful of maximizing investments and minimizing costs. He didn't blink when he said he will receive a six-figure check every month for the rest of his life, though many former champions did; I did too when I found out he earned two million dollars for merely mentioning two sponsors in the post-fight interview. At the close of the press conference, a minion off-camera handed him a Hublot watch. He deftly slipped it around his wrist, on-camera, and walked away from the podium.

His words should echo in the ears of every aspiring boxer in every gym: "I have all my faculties. I invested my money extremely well."

Sometimes you'll see them at night, pitched forward and shuffling along under a street light. Behind them is cast the shadow of the brawler they used to be.

Behind them is Mayweather, watching them go.

He resolved long ago not to follow.

May 4, 2015

Chemin des brumes II by David Senechal

ABOVE THE RAFTERS

Where Have You Gone,
Harry Greb?

Black clouds gather fast and break over Forbes Field in Pittsburgh where Tommy Gibbons (51-0) and Harry Greb (159-12) are fighting like hell. It's the last day of July in 1920 and the crowd is scattering for shelter in the electrical storm. Thunder crashes above the two drenched fighters and Gibbons, standing over six feet tall with a twenty pound weight advantage, lands his feared right cross flush on the jaw of Greb in the seventh round. It doesn't faze the smaller man. Greb is Greb —he's all over Gibbons from every angle, with punch stats off the charts. The lone reporter who had not taken cover under the ring strains to see through the downpour and yells the particulars as his peers scribble away in wet notebooks: "Greb lands a right to the face, a left to the stomach, a right to the ear, a left to the face, a right to the neck." To Gibbons, lightning seems to strike at every angle.

Fifty years later, Francis B. Maloy would recall that the fight was "eerie . . . like a scene from Dante."

Two days earlier, Greb was at Jack Dempsey's training camp in New York City where he fought his third exhibition in three days with the heavyweight champion. Dempsey, known for sending sparring partners out of the ring sideways, could not handle the man known as the "Pittsburgh Windmill" despite being twenty-five pounds heavier and four inches taller. The last day of sparring ended after only two rounds, after their heads collided and Dempsey's eye swelled up.

In September, Dempsey was preparing for an upcoming fight with Billy Miske. Heavyweight "Big" Bill Tate and middleweights Greb and Marty Farrell were his sparring partners. According to the *Pittsburgh Gazette-Times*, "the bout with Greb was a real one … a real honest to goodness battle." Greb was described as a "veritable whirlwind" swarming all over the champion and "forcing him around the ring." Dempsey was throwing his famous short left hooks and rights but could neither connect nor keep him off. Greb hit him as he liked, at times leaping off the canvas to reach his head.

As the curtain descended on 1920, Greb faced "Captain" Bob Roper at the Mechanics Building in Boston. Roper was a journeyman heavyweight known for hard punching and hard ways. With a skull and crossbones befittingly patched onto black trunks, he was disqualified four times in his career and once entered the ring with a live snake around his neck. Despite the presence in his corner of Jack Blackburn (whom Greb had already defeated and who went on to train Joe Louis), Roper did not land more than a half dozen shots on Greb, whose speed and activity was dizzying. *The Boston Daily Globe* described it as "laughable at times"; Roper stretching his neck away from overhands that landed anyway; Roper covering his face with both hands as a "sea of gloves" came at him. It was vintage Greb.

Two years later Greb would fight Tommy Gibbons again at Madison Square Garden. Since the loss to Greb at Forbes Field, Gibbons had earned twenty-one stoppages in twenty-six consecutive victories. The winner of this bout would fight Gene Tunney for the American Light Heavyweight title as a qualifying test to face Dempsey. Seated amid high society were the interested parties: Tunney and Dempsey. More than fourteen thousand had come out to see Gibbons, prematurely decreed as "Dempsey's next opponent." Hundreds of women in evening dress raised the eyebrows of the boys from the Bowery and the Lower East Side and their cheers commingled as "society cast aside all aloofness."

They watched the wrong man win.

Gibbons took only three out of the fifteen rounds. The betting figure that favored him was two-to-one, though the ratio by which he was out-landed in the fight was far beyond that. "I never saw so many boxing gloves in my life," he admitted the next day. "His punches seemed to come from everywhere —from the gallery, from under my shoes, from behind my back."

In May the handicappers around Madison Square Garden got smart and made Greb a three-to-one favorite when he entered the ring against Tunney. Tunney, undefeated before this fight and never defeated again, could not halt the "human hurricane" either, despite being warned by Dempsey himself about Greb's uncanny abilities. According to the *New York Times*, Tunney's exceptional defensive skills were overwhelmed by the attack and he was "completely at sea for fifteen rounds." Greb fractured Tunney's nose in two places and soon rearranged his handsome features into a Picasso painting. His corner ran out of adrenaline chloride to stop the bleeding from his nose, mouth, and two deep cuts over his eyes. An associate sitting ringside sprinted to a druggist for more and cuffed it to Doc Bagley, Tunney's chief second. It didn't matter. Tunney would report that all he saw for most of the fight was a "red phantom," and that Greb "was never in one spot for more than half a second. All my punches were aimed and timed properly but they always wound up hitting empty air. He'd jump in and out, slamming me with a left and then whirling me around with his right or the other way around."

Tunney lost every round.

Dempsey ducked Greb. He fought Gibbons the year after Greb whipped him, and would later twice lose to Tunney, the second time in the famous "Long Count Fight." Greb had been calling out Dempsey almost as soon as the heavyweight began making waves in 1918; he stepped up the pressure after knocking out Gunboat Smith in one round the year after Dempsey knocked him out in two. By June 1922, Greb's manager showed up at Dempsey's manager's office with a generous proposition. It went nowhere. Curiously,

Dempsey chose to fight heavyweights that Greb had already defeated, including not only Gibbons and Tunney, but Miske and "KO" Bill Brennan. Greb was 2-0-1 against Miske and Brennan couldn't beat him to save his life, losing all four bouts against him inside of one year. Earlier in their careers, they shared several opponents. Among them was Willie Meehan whom Greb defeated twice despite a weight disadvantage of thirty pounds. Dempsey posted two losses to Meehan within the same time frame.

"The bigger they are the less respect Harry had for them," Tunney said. "I have seen him virtually climb opponents a foot taller and bring them down to his size." As late as August 1925, Dempsey was still ducking the five-feet-eight middleweight, claiming that the only "fight he wanted was with Harry Wills," who was a six-feet-two, two-hundred-thirteen-pound African-American heavyweight. Dempsey never faced Wills either, though pursued by him as well.

At the end of the Greb-Tunney fight, Tunney collapsed and had to be carried into his dressing room. Stubbornly refusing to go to the hospital, doctors on the scene stitched up his face, reset his nose, and used a stomach pump to remove about two quarts of blood, brandy, orange juice, and adrenaline chloride. Greb, unmarked, didn't look like he even had a fight. He spent the night drinking his beverage of choice, ginger ale, in a speakeasy surrounded by friends.

Happy Albacker was among them. Happy had a secret, but secrets are hard to keep when you're three sheets to the wind. When the inevitable glass was raised and someone toasted Greb's victory "though handicapped by height, weight, and reach," Albacker blurted out "—and by one eye!" Had it not been for Greb's ability to parry unexpected blows, the secret would have been out. It would have meant the end of his career.

Greb's vision in his right eye had been diminishing since the summer of 1921, when Kid Norfolk thumbed him during a particularly violent match in Pittsburgh. Bill Paxton, author of *The Fearless Harry Greb* offers compelling evidence that he suffered a retinal tear in the Norfolk fight and so had only partial vision when he defeated Gibbons, Tunney, and Tommy Loughran (incidentally, three of the greatest light heavyweights of all time). Paxton believes that he went completely blind in his right eye following his fifth fight with Captain Bob Roper. He took almost two months off, spent a week in the hospital, and was seen with patches over both eyes.

His return to the ring was on New Year's Day, 1923 —against Captain Bob Roper.

He would fight sixty-eight more times, take the middleweight title and defend it six times, defeat future middleweight champions Tiger Flowers and Mickey Walker, and master Jimmy Slattery and Maxie Rosenbloom, all while blind in one eye.

According to the *Boston Daily Globe*, Greb earned a few technical knockouts in Pittsburgh one night, though unofficially. After a female companion in his car was relieved of ninety-five dollars and a ring on a lonely road in Highland Park by five robbers, Greb reported the incident to the police. When they arrived on the scene, the officers noticed blood all over the road. It wasn't Greb's.

Moved at the ensuing hearing by the weeping wife and children of one of the assailants, Greb offered to post bail. For those close to him, this was not a surprise. Contrary to the myth that he was a half-cocked hell-raiser, Greb was a kind man and a practicing Roman Catholic. There is nothing to suggest that he was anything less than in love with his wife Mildred throughout their courtship and marriage. When she died of tuberculosis on March 18, 1923 he was at her bedside. And it is to his immortal credit that he had no regard for color lines. Some boxing historians rightfully attach an asterisk to the accolades of Dempsey, Tunney, and Loughran because they would not fight the full range of threats on the spectrum. Neither Tunney nor Loughran ever faced an African American over the length of their professional careers.

Greb, by contrast, avoided no man.

As early as 1915 he faced Jack Blackburn and would accept the challenges of several other black fighters before he was finished, including Willie Langford, Kid Norfolk, Kid Lewis, Allentown Joe

Gans, and Tiger Flowers.

Greb's final appearance in the ring was in 1926. It was an attempt to regain the middleweight crown he lost to Flowers. The handicapped ex-champion turned the clock back and fought well in losing a second decision to Flowers. Most believed that the victory was rightfully his, that he had done more than enough to take back the title. Greb himself was adamant. "Well," he said, "that was one fight I won if I ever won any."

But the windmill was creaking.

In September, his right eye was surgically removed and replaced with a glass one. He confided to a friend that his career was over and that he planned to open a gym in downtown Pittsburgh. It must have been bittersweet as he sat in the audience at the Dempsey-Tunney bout in Philadelphia later that month. He watched Tunney do what he always knew he himself could do if given the opportunity: outbox Dempsey and become the heavyweight champion of the world.

The end was near. After an operation to repair damage sustained in his latest car accident, he fell into a coma. At 2:30 p.m. on October 22, 1926, the former middleweight king died of heart failure. The news shocked the boxing world.

This fighter's fighter, often seen smiling in the heat of battle and laughing when hit with a good shot, lived only two months after his final bout. Perhaps he was a romantic who couldn't live without the object of his passion. This much is beyond dispute: in a rougher era when boxing was just emerging from the seedy underground and men fought to live, Greb lived to fight.

His legend dwarfs what we see today. In a career that spanned from 1913 to 1926 and over three hundred fights, he overwhelmed fifteen Hall of Famers and a dozen world champions in four divisions. Ninety years ago, he gave us a boxing milestone that you can bet your house will never be repeated. Greb fought forty-five times in 1919. That's an average of one bout every eight days against an array of sluggers, boxer-punchers, and defensive specialists. That's a record of 45-0 against not only other middleweights, but light heavyweights and heavyweights in one calendar year.

So what are you waiting for? Raise a glass of ginger ale in honor of the Pittsburgh Windmill —a remarkable middleweight who fought them all, any time, any place; the restless spirit behind every club fighter, contender, and champion who fights with the sudden, ruthless passion of a summer storm.

Here's to you, Harry Greb.

May 3, 2009

Boston Beats the Count

Edwin "La Bomba" Rodriguez, a super-middleweight contender living in Massachusetts, sparred with Tamerlan Tsarnaev two years ago. "Today I find out he's a terrorist and one of the Boston Marathon bombers," he posted on his Facebook page last Friday. "I'm glad I put a beating on him, but wish I'd known he was evil, because I wouldn't have slowed down on him."

According to USA Boxing, Tsarnaev was registered in Massachusetts as an amateur boxer in 2004-2005 and in 2008-2010. He trained at the Somerville Boxing Gym and later at the South Boston Boxing Club. Apparently his first amateur fight was at the Golden Gloves competition at Lowell Memorial Auditorium in January 2004. The Lowell Sun reported that he arrived in the United States and settled in Cambridge only five months earlier. His family had fled Grozny, Chechnya, which was ground zero in the Russo-Chechen wars of the mid-1990s and the early part of the twenty-first century. In 2003, the United Nations called it "the most destroyed city on earth."

To Tsarnaev, the Golden Gloves marked a new beginning. "I like the USA," he told the *Sun*. "You have a chance to make money here if you are willing to work." "I think he can win the whole thing," his trainer said after that first bout. "He can throw." The trainer in the opposite corner was just as impressed. "There might not be a better fighter in the [light heavyweight] class. He was good."

Tsarnaev was good enough to fight his way into the 2009 National Golden Gloves Championship's heavyweight class at Salt Lake City. He knocked down his Chicagoan opponent only to lose what was called a controversial decision. The next year he won the New England regional tournament and the prestigious Rocky Marciano Trophy. He was supposed to represent New England in the Nationals again, but was disqualified when it was discovered that he was not yet an American citizen.

Trainer Kendrick Ball remembers the first time he saw Tsarnaev. "He was wearing a white shirt unbuttoned, tight jeans, and a trench coat. His shoes were bright like aluminum foil." He had "a swagger," Ball recalled. He seemed to be inviting someone to clown him but the trainer soon realized "he could back it up." Working the opposite corner, Ball watched him throw jabs up from the waist with a sharp exhale "like a steam shovel," and follow up with powerful right hands. "He was strong," Ball said, strong enough to invite to Camp Get Right (Ball's gym in Worcester) for sparring. So the trainer and the fighter exchanged numbers and set dates.

Tsarnaev showed up to spar —alone. No trainer came with him, no second. And that's a no-no in boxing. "I would never send my fighters to spar at another gym without me," Ball said. "You never know what can happen. They can be overmatched; suffer a concussion that you might never hear about." Stranger still was the fact that Tsarnaev brought no mouth piece, protective cup, or headgear. When Ball offered to let him borrow equipment, Tsarnaev declined. "He told me that's how he fights."

Ball let him go four rounds with an amateur light heavyweight, who dropped him with a left hook to the ribs. Tsarnaev recovered and wanted to continue. Ball wouldn't let him. Instead, he invited him to spar with a super middleweight currently ranked ninth by the *Transnational Boxing Rankings*. "Edwin [Rodriguez] is too small for me," Tsarnaev said. "I'll take it easy on him." Ball chuckled at that, and told him to "watch Friday Night Fights and see if you need to take it easy on him." (Rodriguez scored a first round knockout on

March 19, 2010 in a televised bout.) Tsarnaev watched, unmoved. "I'll take it easy on him," he said again.

In boxing parlance, "a gentleman" is a fighter who can be counted on to take it easy when sparring a lesser opponent. Rodriguez is "a gentleman," said Ball —unless provoked. Tsarnaev's arrogance provoked him.

Tsarnaev went two rounds with Rodriguez, who had no problem solving that steam-shovel jab and landing at will. Tsarnaev was too hurt to continue on for a third round, but soon recovered and insisted on going back in for more. Rodriguez decided to teach him a hard lesson. Before the round was over, Tsarnaev left the ring holding his side and spitting up blood in a bucket. Ball later found out that Rodriguez had broken one of his ribs. Afterwards, Tsarnaev had a more realistic outlook. "Edwin is really good," he admitted.

Tsarnaev and his half-empty gym bag traveled to different clubs around Massachusetts looking for sparring. Ex-middleweight contender Rodney Toney, now a trainer, saw him at The Ring Boxing Club on Commonwealth Ave on a couple of occasions. The Ring is located near the route of the Boston Marathon.

In 2010, Tsarnaev was pursuing his dream to fight for the United States Olympic Team.

By 2011, his dream was fraying. According to FBI records, a foreign government petitioned them about him. The request was "based on information that he was a follower of radical Islam and a strong believer, and that he had changed drastically since 2010." The FBI conducted a background check and interviewed the young man but found no evidence of terrorist activity.

In the summer of 2011, Tsarnaev showed up at the Big Six Boxing Academy in Providence. As usual, he was alone. Jason "Big Six" Estrada, a professional heavyweight tipping the scales at over two hundred thirty pounds, sparred with him on two occasions and noticed that the stranger fought in a stand-up, European style with his lead arm extended out and both hands waving around probing for an opening. Estrada said that he had decent speed and a good defense, though it wasn't enough: Estrada dropped him with body shots. Tsarnaev kept getting up and "coming back hard." They sparred two sessions before it was decided to put him in with a fighter his own size. That fighter, a cruiserweight with twelve professional fights, was expected to handle the amateur. "I'm not gonna lie," Estrada told me. "Tamerlan made him look silly."

An opportunity beckoned. Big Six Entertainment was planning to promote its first professional card in December 2011. Tsarnaev "wanted to get on that card," Estrada said. "And we were more than willing to get him on that card."

But Tsarnaev never got back to him.

That may have been the pivot that changed the trajectory of his life. Tsarnaev drifted away from the boxing ring and into something else, something dark. Travel records indicate that he left the U.S. in January 2012 and took a flight to Sheretmetyevo International Airport in Russia. He returned in July, wearing a beard.

There are reports on the New England boxing circuit suggesting that his interest in boxing sputtered into this year before it died. Only two months ago, Kendrick Ball bumped into him at Lowell's Golden Gloves tournament. "We talked boxing for about fifteen minutes," Ball said. "I was going to call him in the next few weeks to spar with my fighter."

Ball and Estrada were stunned at the news that he may have been responsible for taking four lives, including a child's, and maiming over a hundred spectators and participants at the Boston Marathon. "He could've turned professional," Ball said, his voice dropping to a whisper. "He would've been somebody we'd hear about, in a good way." Could he have been a contender? Estrada believes he would have been "a crowd-pleaser."

Imagine that.

America is no longer secure. Our dialogue with the world has changed over the past twenty years and our enemies have changed as well. The existential threat that tried to erase the world's oldest monotheistic religion and saw bomb shelters built in backyards has been turned on its head. Where Nazism and communism perverted reason and tried to break the moorings of faith, the new threat perverts faith and considers reason a sin.

Throughout its history, Boston has been the nation's plain-speaking conscience, pointing toward both faith and reason when things get unruly. When patriots dumped British tea in the harbor, we told our sister colonies that it was high time for independence, and they followed. The abolitionist movement of the next century also found its epicenter here; years before the Civil War, Boston said it was high time that slavery ended, and the rest followed or were dragged. Ours is a city of callused hands, strong virtue, and beginnings. It is no wonder that the first professional police department was established here, as was the first free public library.

Last Monday Tsarnaev and his brother walked down Boylston Street in the shade of that library. It is alleged that they were behind what happened next, a terrorist attack during a sacred event. The city acted with the discipline of the Puritans who founded it. It shut itself down to make damn sure whoever did it got what was coming to them. All day Friday, the brownstones themselves seemed to glare in the eerie stillness; and the moment the faces of the bombers were broadcast to the world, a million eyes scanned the city and surrounding areas.

The Tsarnaev brothers grew desperate. They shot and killed a Massachusetts Institute of Technology officer in cold blood, carjacked an SUV, and were chased by screaming blue lights across Watertown. They threw bombs out the window to slow down their pursuers but were cornered on Dexter Street. A firefight erupted in a residential neighborhood.

Tamerlan Tsarnaev madly flung himself toward the police officers with an explosive device strapped to his chest. He was shot to pieces. His injured brother was found curled up in a boat by a streetwise citizen. He is now in custody under heavy guard at Mount Auburn Hospital.

On April 19, 1897 the first Boston Marathon was run. On April 15, 2013 there was blood at the finish line of the one hundred seventeenth. We'll clean it up, take care of our own and anyone else who comes here with good intentions, and run again next year.

This is a place of beginnings, not endings. On April 15, 2013 a baby was born to boxing contender and gentleman Edwin Rodriguez. His name is Evan.

April 21, 2013

Somebody Up There

I'm neither saint nor sinner. I'm a gladiator.
—Sugar Ray Robinson

Two thousand years ago, the bell summoning gladiators to ring center wasn't a bell at all. It was a long, hollow blast from an ancient Roman wind instrument called a tibia. The tibia was also heard during public sacrifices and funerals, much like bells today are used in church and as a death toll.

The crowd's roar at the Flavian Amphitheater is still heard at the MGM Grand. It is an echo in time. Virgil's words echo with it:
Now, let any man with heart,
with the fire in his chest, come forward —
put up his fists, strap on the rawhide gloves.

The Roman poet's words are found in the *Aeneid*, which was written between 29 and 19 BC. Today, they dominate a wall at Gleason's Gym in Brooklyn.

The fighter comes forward like he always has, struggling to do unto his opponent what his opponent intends to do unto him — and do it first. Hand-wringing humanists needn't look much further to support their argument for boxing's abolition, the strongest of which is not that it is the most dangerous sport, but that the intention of its participants is to inflict harm ("clean punching" is the first of the four typical criteria judges use to score a round). That is what separates boxing from other sports, including mixed martial arts. Although the injury rate in the so-called "savage science" exceeds boxing's, head trauma is less frequent in the octagon because there are more options to end matters early. Submission holds appear brutal, but they are, in fact, safer than a knockout. The beset MMA fighter need only "tap-out" to end his suffering. The beset boxer has no such option. He'd be better off letting an official halt the fight or just take one on the chin, because to quit would invite a scarlet letter for the rest of his life.

Ray Arcel's career as a trainer spanned seven decades. "Only once," he recalled, "did I have a fighter tell me he wanted to quit; he said, 'I'm gonna quit this round.' I said, 'You can't. There are people here. They paid to see these fights.'" Arcel lifted him off the stool and sent him out round after round. His fighter would not quit; instead he kept maneuvering the opponent's back to the corner. "Ray!" he'd yell over a shoulder. "Trow in the towel!"

Boxing's culture is not only older than the MMA's, it's tougher. It has spawned a mythos closest to the gladiator's in ancient Rome, compelling the boxer to wade into danger when he knows he won't win and to get up when he can't. There are haunting images of fighters who should have quit and ended up half-conscious on their stools slipping invisible shots after the fight is called off, or laid out flat on the canvas with their eyelids fluttering, still punching up at the lights. The mythos lies heavily across shoulders rarely broad enough to uphold it. Sometimes something snaps. Four days before Bob Olin was scheduled to defend his light heavyweight crown against John Henry Lewis, Arcel walked into his hotel room and found him standing there with his pants on over his pajamas and wearing an overcoat. "I'm gonna die, I'm gonna die," Olin moaned. "I don't know what's the matter with me. I'm gonna die." Arcel put him to bed and got him warm milk. "I stroked his hands and his forehead," he said, "and talked to him like he was a baby."

One of the best boxing analysts in the business today is Teddy Atlas. Trainer, author, humanitarian, and commentator on ESPN's *Friday Night Fights,* Atlas understands the mythos. He holds that the boxer is not as secure as assumed; that he is insecure because he is acting against his own instincts for self-preservation and is doing something "unnatural."

Fear is there, always. Novices bar the door and veterans perfect the poker-face but the chill creeps in anyway, and builds. "You know, fighters don't tell you they're afraid," Arcel said. "They don't try to tell you what's going on inside of them. They lose their food in the dressing room, and they'll say it must have been something they ate." Leaving the dressing room is the worst. Draped in a robe that feels like a shroud, the boxer's walk to the ring, trainer in tow, feels something like a condemned man's walk to the death chamber, priest in tow.

Some fighters distract themselves with feigned bravura. Others surround themselves with familiars like security blankets. Ethnic garb is donned. Patriotic music blares. When Holman Williams walked toward a Baltimore ring to face his *bête noir* Cocoa Kid in 1940, Joe Louis and Jack Blackburn came with him. As if that wasn't enough, a mysterious symbol was stitched on the front of his robe and the words "I WILL" were on the back. In recent years, gangsta rappers have accompanied champions on the way to the ring to fill their ears with courage. (Bubblegum Justin Bieber followed Floyd Mayweather Jr. recently though the point of that was lost on me.) Older boxing fans will recall a premier fighter who performed his own rap on the way to dispense with yet another mid-career soft touch. What they may not recall is that this tendency began after a rival ended up blind and disabled in a wheelchair.

It isn't hard to understand, really. The truth of existence has a way of coming into focus when you're flat on your back under the lights and there's nowhere to look but up. Whether those lights are in an arena, a nursing home, or on a Chicago street is beside the point; we'll all see them eventually. In this sense, the boxer is a proxy preparing the way for all of us. He takes self-reliance as far as it will go and finds it's not enough. Advanced skill is canceled out by a badly-timed blink as easily as the power of positive thinking is cancelled out by the Grim Reaper. It's an awful truth. Pop culture has it all wrong; our fate, ultimately, is not in our hands. It's a roll of the dice, a game of chance, blind luck.

Or is it?

The two best fighters today don't consider themselves lucky; they consider themselves blessed. After super-middleweight king Andre Ward stopped light-heavyweight king Chad Dawson, he was asked about the risks involved. "Give me five seconds," Ward interrupted. "I want to thank my Lord and Savior Jesus Christ and all the people that's been praying for me leading up to this fight." After Mayweather defeated Robert Guerrero, he said, "First off, I'd like to thank God for this victory."

Character flaws don't block the view. The most flawed among us tend to get knocked flat more than the rest and so don't have to crank our heads to look up. Roberto Duran reached the peak of his spiteful splendor when he defeated Sugar Ray Leonard, only to fall from the sky like Lucifer when he quit the rematch. He was surging again in 1983 when he found himself in the ring with middleweight king and three-to-one favorite Marvin Hagler; an ominous challenge bigger and stronger than anything he had ever faced this side of a horse. Just before the opening bell rang, Duran did something uncharacteristic —he crossed himself.

The praying boxer has been a motif at least since the modern era began in 1920. And it seems that those who spent the least time on their knees in the ring spent the most time on their knees out of it. Harry Greb was a member of the Pittsburgh Lyceum, which was founded by a Roman Catholic priest who later presided over his marriage. Greb himself was a devout Catholic who donated thousands to his parish and rarely boxed or trained on Sundays. His successor to the middleweight throne was Tiger Flowers. Flowers was known as "the Deacon" and told the *Atlanta Constitution* that he took time after every fight to "thank God for the strength that brought me through." When Ezzard Charles defeated Joe Louis, he said what his grandmother told him to say: "I'd like to give thanks to God for giving me the strength and courage to win the fight." After

Henry Armstrong took the second of three simultaneous divisional crowns, he walked into a Harlem club to celebrate. As the club manager fawned over him he felt "a strange touch on his shoulder." He said it was God. After that, he made it a point to go off alone after his fights to pray. He was ordained a Baptist minister in 1951 and wrote an autobiography called *Gloves, Glory, and God*.

Sugar Ray Robinson was no exception. "I believe that of himself man can do nothing," he said. "He needs God to guide him and bless him." When Robinson first retired from the ring and tried show business, he made an oath to stay retired. "I intend to keep it," he told a Franciscan priest in 1955, despite the fact that his new venture was an utter failure. "But I'm thousands behind. I want to pay my bills, but I can't if I'm a hoofer." Father Jovian Lang assured him that his boxing talent was a gift from his Maker and that it was all right to return to the ring. With the fighter on his knees, the priest gave him a blessing to protect him from harm, and by the end of the year, Sugar Ray was preparing to challenge the middleweight champion to reclaim his old crown. A reporter was in the dressing room twenty minutes before the fight. He noted that everyone walked lightly and spoke softly "almost as if they were at a funeral" while the fighter sucked an ice cube and paced to and fro like a man awaiting execution. The reporter was surprised to see him kiss a silver crucifix that was pinned to the inside of his trunks.

Sugar Ray scored a knockout in the fourth round, and broke down and cried all the way to the dressing room.

Two years later, he lost the title to Gene Fullmer and was training for the rematch when that old familiar fear overtook him. Father Jovian received a "distress call" from his wife. Sugar Ray "was tied up in knots," he recalled. "His confidence had begun to waver." The priest and the thirty-six-year-old pugilist had several private sessions in the weeks leading up to the fight. When the priest noted that the bout would be on May 1, the feast of St. Joseph the Worker, he added an intercessory prayer to that saint.

At Chicago Stadium on the night of the fight, a figure in a long brown robe kept shouting "Go to *work*, Ray! Go to *work*!" from a seat behind the Robinson corner. It was Father Jovian.

That thunderbolt of a left hook that Sugar Ray landed in the fifth round was a study in efficiency. It was set up on the retreat, knocked Fullmer out, and is remembered as one of the most perfect punches ever landed. It began his fourth reign on the middleweight throne and confirmed his status as one of history's greatest gladiators.

And as the crowds filed out of Chicago Stadium and well-wishers filed into his dressing room, an AP reporter noticed that a sense of wonder seemed to have overtaken the new champion. "Somebody up there likes you," the reporter said.

"He sure does," Sugar Ray said, looking up. "He's got His arm around me."

July 22, 2013

Zimmerman, Boxing, and Civic Duty

No winner can rightfully be declared after *The State of Florida v. George Zimmerman*. It was a tragedy that became a fiasco after it was hijacked by an irresponsible media that longs to see a house divided.

The *New York Times* set the tone. It shrugged off the killer's Peruvian identity and called him a "white Hispanic" and so reduced the fourth estate to a schoolyard instigator. The President — who won't be referred to as a "white African American" though his mother was as white as Zimmerman's father— has been intimately involved. As a matter of law, it is settled: Zimmerman shot and killed Trayvon Martin in an act the jury determined was self-defense. But it isn't over. The victim was brought up in the New York mayoral race just yesterday; outrage floods the internet; and protests continue in urban communities, including Chicago, where the reverends are wondering where the spotlight is when it comes to harsher realities like black-on-black murder.

At the center of it all is a quiet grave in Dade Memorial Park and a forgotten truth: a young man is dead and America is poorer for it.

Martin was one of our own. A child of divorce, a good to middling student who wanted to work in aviation as a pilot or mechanic, a recreational drug user, and a cell phone addict. He was also a six-feet-one-inch seventeen-year-old who liked to fight.

Zimmerman, and every other "Zimmerman" in the new America, would do well to learn how to fight.

Deadly Force

According to the U.S. Justice Department, murders committed with a gun dropped 39% over the past twenty years. Other crimes committed with a gun dropped 69% during the same period. Possible explanations include lower birth rates, a combination of proactive policing and long-term incarceration of chronic violent offenders, more social programs and government assistance, and the so-called "graying of America" (violent crime, like boxing, is a young man's activity).

Few experts attribute the decline to private gun ownership, which has doubled since 1968. The U.S. leads the world in guns per capita, according to a survey conducted by a Swiss research group. It's no contest. The American rate of gun ownership is three times Canada's and six times México's. In real numbers, there are over three hundred ten million legally owned guns across the land of the free, and sales are up.

That's a problem.

The U.S. remains one of the most violent industrialized nations on the planet. And make no mistake: our natural propensities are made that much worse because our guns are within reach. The National Rifle Association disputes this and stands on the assertion that gun ownership is the mark of a patriot. It spotlights examples of crime prevention by licensed guns as much as the mainstream media buries them. The NRA's Institute for Legislative Action website invites supporters to contribute stories about the heroics of the "Armed Citizen" protecting person and property. Thus far this summer, there have been eleven entries.

But the facts shoot back. The Bureau of Justice Statistics found that "less than 1% of non-fatal violent crime victims reported using a gun to defend themselves." Meanwhile, the likelihood of suicide, lethal domestic violence, and accidental deaths increase dramatically when a gun is in the house. Homicide and "unintentional gun fatality" rates are off the charts, and they are especially bad in areas with more privately owned guns and less gun control.

The NRA has an image problem. The USA has an image problem. An enduring one is that of the square-jawed American carrying a musket with one foot on a rock. It hearkens back to the Revolutionary War, when British soldiers invaded these shores and the call went out to every able-bodied colonist for the defense of hearth and home. The second amendment is a tribute to that image. What happened on the night of February 26, 2012 in Sanford, Florida is not.

Boxing: A Civic Duty?

Able-bodied citizens in a first world country should not need to carry a firearm to feel safe. Simply stated, self-defense is an absolute right; overkill is not. More simply stated, if George Zimmerman knew how to use his fists he would have spared the life of a teenager and prevented a media-driven frenzy.

Zimmerman was described by a witness for the defense as "a very nice person, but not a fighter." Dennis Root, an expert in the use of force testified that he considers several factors when examining self-defense cases including gender, age, size, physical abilities, and special circumstances that can figure into such situations. Particular emphasis is placed on background and training, and for good reason. When a person finds him or herself under attack, the immediate question is whether the person is equipped to repel the attack.

When presented with the defense's version of events that said Zimmerman was punched in the nose and then mounted and pummeled before shooting his attacker, Root had this to say: "I don't know what else he could do based on his abilities ... not to be offensive to Mr. Zimmerman, but he doesn't seem to have any."

Years ago, I was hitting the speed bag in the basement boxing room of the Boston YMCA when a grey-headed trainer approached. The trainer's name was Pete Cone. "Three hoodlums just tried to rob me," he said. He was well into his fifties at the time and took care of his housebound mother. He had an easy smile, a twinkle in his eye, and was so soft-spoken you'd have to lean in to hear him. I heard him. "Whoa! Whoa!" I said. "You all right? Where are they?" Pete said, "I'm fine, just fine. I managed to knock two of them down but the third one, well, he ran away and I just couldn't catch up to him." It should be mentioned that Pete was also an ex-fighter who once fought an exhibition with the late, great Emile Griffith.

The sweet science is a social hub for stories like this, and they're not hard to substantiate:

• Last year, an eighty-four-year-old former fighter named Peter Sandy was walking to a Tesco store in Cambridge, England when a mugger pulled a commando-style knife on him. According to *Mail Online*, Sandy threw a left hook and the mugger fell to the ground. "When he recovered, he ran off." Sandy said. "The punch was instinctive. I used to train for six hours a day and in that moment it all came back to me." He retired fifty-six years ago. The article is entitled "You Picked the Wrong Guy!"

• Rossie Ellis was a middle-aged ex-boxer when he was stabbed in the arm with an ice pick. According to the *Hartford Courant*, he turned around and knocked out the man who did it.

• Last October, the *Telegraph* reported that Amir Khan and his brother, also a professional boxer, fought six men when they tried to steal his Range Rover. One of the attackers took a swing at Amir, who was three months removed from his third career loss, and was knocked cold when Amir pulled back and countered. The other five went down like Whac-A-Moles.

• In Oklahoma City last December, a young man broke into the garage of a boxer, took a swing at him, and ended up taking the beating of his life. The young man's mug shot says it all: both eyes swelled shut and gauze stuffed up his nose and in his lip. The *Blaze* entitled the article "This Is Why You Never, Ever Break Into a Boxer's Home."

• In Manhattan in 1969, a well-dressed elderly gentleman sat in the back of a taxi stopped at a red light. He spied two "young punks" running toward the doors on either side. While the driver sat terrified, his fare clambered out and "flattened both" with a right cross for one and a left hook for the other. Two unofficial knockouts can be added to the record of Jack Dempsey.

These types of confrontations are everyday occurrences or close to it. Most go unrecorded though the result is the same —no one had to die.

When Zimmerman joined the Kokopelli Gym in Longwood, Florida, he was obese. He did a commendable job losing weight and signed up for a boxing class. At his free trial, gym owner Adam Pollock testified that he was considerably "nonathletic" and never advanced beyond shadow boxing and working the heavy bag. "He didn't know how to effectively punch," Pollock said, though the fault of that would lie with the trainer, not a willing client.

An advertisement for the Kokopelli boxing program asserts that "transferring energy to a specific target is a skill that ANYONE can learn providing they have the right coaching." It goes on to invite clients to "learn to hit with POWER regardless of gender, size or age" and "develop practical defensive fundamentals like catching, parrying, redirecting and leverage stopping."

Pollock made it clear that in his gym, novices are not allowed to spar until they develop the requisite skill. Zimmerman never developed the requisite skill. However, he also took a grappling class and managed to advance enough to work with a partner.

"It's very important to understand the difference between the two concepts," Root testified. "[I]n grappling you have the opportunity to what we call 'tap out'. You can say 'I quit' [or] 'I give up' if something hurts too much." Not so in boxing. "In boxing," Root said, "when you enter the ring with another person, you find you've entered into too much, you know, more than you can handle when you've been punched and injured already."

It is an important differentiation.

It is nearly certain that a fight between Zimmerman and Martin took place on the grounds of the Twin Lakes gated community. The defense presented a narrative that placed Zimmerman outside of his vehicle looking for an address to assist police in locating what he believed was a suspicious person. When Zimmerman proceeded back to his vehicle, Martin supposedly appeared and said "What the f*ck's your problem, homie?" Zimmerman replied, "Hey man, I don't have a problem." Martin approached with a balled fist and said "you have a problem now!"

Even if we accept the defense's version of events, an incident that begins with a conk on the nose should not end with a call to the coroner, particularly if the intended victim is an able-bodied male.

Had Zimmerman been trained properly and/or taken boxing more seriously, he could have slipped the first blow and countered it with his own. He might have countered the blow with a six-punch combination like the great Peruvian light heavyweight Mauro Mina, the "Bombardero de Chincha." Who knows.

We know this much: the sweet science is extraordinarily effective in the street. It breeds confidence, teaches self-control, sharpens the senses, and has been proven viable for self-defense long past physical primes. It can cancel out disadvantages in size and flab and it gives citizens something to hold on to, something other than cold steel. A well-schooled left hook is enough to dissuade most anyone from bad intentions. There is no need to kill anyone. Let him get up, wipe the red off his face with his sleeve, and stumble on his way. Once his head clears he'll have new manners to think about.

The iconic image of the stalwart American proudly bearing a firearm is selling us short. For a people who have historically prided themselves on self-reliance and skill, why bring a gun to a fist fight? Patriots shouldn't and true tough guys wouldn't. The end result is only trauma for victim, shooter, and everyone around them. We just witnessed how traumatic it can be for the whole country.

There are a hundred forty-nine handgun ranges and a hundred sixty-nine boxing gyms in Florida.

Neither is hard to find.

July 30, 2013

Joe

Stillman's Gym, 1947. Rocky Graziano was cutting figure eights in front of a drumming speed bag with a Chesterfield on the edge of his lip. It was lit, but that was damn-near expected at smoky Stillman's. It was damn-near appreciated too, given the stench the joint was famous for. An eleven-year-old boy sauntered up to the fighter. His name was Joe Rein and he was playing hooky. After a while, Graziano looked down.

"Why ain't you in school?" he said.

"—Why ain't YOU!"

Graziano, Joe recalled, "roared with laughter" and hoisted him up on his shoulders. He was introduced to a gallery of kings and contenders and before the stars were out of his eyes he was on a first-name basis with all of them.

Jake LaMotta was introduced to him by Willie Pep. "Kid, you have hands like mine," LaMotta said. "You gotta learn to go to the body." Small-handed and short-armed Joe was taught to slip rights and lefts on both sides to land unexpected counters. "Most fighters are predictable," LaMotta said.

Some of what Joe learned was anything but predictable. Gym wisdom warns against crossing your feet in the ring though Sugar Ray Robinson himself told him that was a myth. Fighters, he said, "should cross their feet sometimes to move more easily." Robinson also showed him a trick to maximize the power of the left hook. He positioned the kid, who was a right-hander, into the southpaw position to throw a right hook, doubling it up to the body and head. He instructed him to throw his left hook the same way, "as it comes," and not to worry about it being textbook. His own left hook was really a half-uppercut, Robinson said, and a slow motion YouTube review of just what it was that tipped over Gene Fullmer affirms it.

Joe "Old Bones" Brown kept the wolves away. When managers came around looking for meat to feed their prospects, Brown wouldn't let the kid in the ring. "He wouldn't let me get smashed at Stillman's," said Joe. Brown thus did a favor to posterity: he helped preserve the golden memory of someone destined to become the golden era's greatest ambassador to the twenty-first century.

Sixty-six years after he was introduced to the greatest fighters who ever lived, Joe was logging on and introducing them to a generation of fans whose parents weren't even born in 1947 and who lived thousands of miles from the site of long-gone Stillman's Gym. Joe was a regular on eastsideboxing.com's forums since August 2004. He posted five thousand nine hundred and nineteen times under the username of a movie star from way back: "John Garfield."

It was no idle choice. Garfield, born in New York City, was a corner kid who found refuge in boxing and friends in low places. He learned his trade in local theater troupes, moved to Hollywood, and took New York with him. In other words, he never went soft. Garfield reached his peak of fame during the Red Scare and was called to testify before the House Committee on Un-American Activities in 1951. He refused to name names and his career took a dive because of it. Joe idolized Garfield for this working class loyalty, for that old-school cool.

In 1952, Joe was fifteen and feeling it. "Makes me cringe at whatta A-hole I musta looked like, Springs," he said. "Amboy Dukes to my toes, DA haircut, Tony Curtis spit curl; high rise, chartreuse pegged pants (12-inch cuffs, 32-inch knees —think MC Hammer), saddle stitching, and pistol pockets. I walked two blocks before my legs moved!"

The actor he loved had a fatal heart attack on May 21, 1952 and was buried twenty miles north of the city in Westchester Hills. But Joe wouldn't let him die.

He sent me a publicity shot of himself doing his best Garfield impression in 1958 and another altogether different one in a gym in the 1970s. "You're Lon Chaney," I quipped about his different looks. He replied: "In '60, Springs, [I] worked on a low-budget anti-Castro feature in Florida with Lon Chaney Jr. and Jake LaMotta. Chaney was such a falling-down drunk he never left the set after a day's shoot, just collapsed in the bushes with a bottle, and that's the way we found him the next morning." I thought that was something until he told me he was flashed by Jane Wyatt of "Father Knows Best" fame.

The first time I watched *Blast of Silence* (1961), an obscure film noir by fellow Brooklynite and Rein-lookalike Allen Baron, I called him up excitedly. Joe must have thought I was cute. "I worked on that film!" he said and reduced me yet again to stunned silence. Another time I told him I was a sucker for easy-listening music and Ed Ames's "My Cup Runneth Over." His response? "Studied with Ed at the John Cassavetes Theater workshop in New York in the early 60s."

Joe was never boastful, never a name-dropper; and, like his idol, he never betrayed a trust. He would share stories matter-of-factly and at times with a twinkle in his eye because he knew they were sure to entertain.

Entertainment was on his mind when he moved out to Los Angeles in the 1970s. Like Garfield, he took New York with him. He produced commercials for an advertisement agency, taught writing classes at UCLA, and kept his hand in boxing. He was a fixture at the Wild Card Gym and wrote fly-on-the-wall articles for The Sweet Science that are classics. He sat ringside for Manny Pacquiao's American debut at the MGM Grand in 2001 and became one of his earliest American believers. By his own admission, he "needed Cruise shoes to be taller than Manny" but he became for him what he was for so many others —an encourager. Ten years later, Joe was diagnosed with cancer and didn't get around much anymore. Pacquiao found out and asked him to sit ringside at Pacquiao-Marquez III, again at the MGM Grand. "There are a million people banging on his door," Joe said. "It's just amazing."

Joe always could spot talent. "You've got the goods," he'd say. When he said it to me in 2009, I listened. I sat down and typed an essay spurred more by his confidence than my own, and sent it to him. He took it like it was the start of something grand and brought it to Michael Woods, editor-in-chief of The Sweet Science, and with that, my life got better. The second boxing essay I wrote was a tribute to my new friend's golden memories. I called it "1949: The Perfect Storm of Pugilism." I should have called it "A Love Letter to Joe Rein."

My encourager never let up. When I wrote The Gods of War, he said I ought to be arrested because it was "more addictive than crack." I told him "The Summer of '42" was among my choices for background music while writing it. "'The Summer of '42' has special meaning for me," he said. "The author, Herman Raucher, was my youth-camp counselor in '47." I threw up my hands.

The last fight I covered thrilled him ("like a Friday night in the 40s when Graziano headlined the ol' MSG… Bless you!"), which thrilled me. "Words are precious to me," he'd say, and barring a hospital stay he never failed to call or email within hours after my latest essay was published. I grew to rely on it. I went and bought a vintage desk phone just to hear him better when he called.

He was the consigliere in my ear for every major decision I've made over the past five years. Despite being housebound, Joe was a guiding spirit behind the Transnational Boxing Rankings and helped navigate what he called "shark-infested waters." When Teddy Atlas mentioned my name and endorsed the new rankings on Friday Night Fights last August, Joe said he "nearly broke the lease cheering so loud …"

I told him he'd always be Seneca to my Nero. "Who ya callin' Sanka?" he shot back.

He loved my 2010 Camaro. Two years ago I sent an email to members of the Boxing Writers Association of America encouraging them to read my series on Cocoa Kid and vote him into the International Boxing Hall of Fame. On the subject line of the email to Joe I wrote, "A Camaro for a vote for Cocoa Kid." His reply: "That you think you can bribe me is OFFENSIVE! Ya can take the Camaro 'n STICK IT in my garage." He got a package from Boston on his next birthday. "Told my wife ta run if the package is ticking," he wrote back. He opened it to find a matchbox-sized Camaro. He roared. "Gonna get a thimble of water," he said, "and polish it up."

My mother went in for high-risk surgery soon after that and Joe was right there, a loyal friend. Knowing I'm Catholic, he sent along a prayer to Mother Mary. "Your mom's gonna be OK," he said. When he spoke, I listened, and as usual, he was right.

Joe's health took a turn for the worse over the past year. He became more introspective. Not long ago, he shared some sentiments that he always tried to live by. One of them put something in my eye: "Friendship isn't about whom you have known the longest. It's about those who came and never left your side."

November 7, 2013. I hadn't heard from my friend in some weeks and my calls went unanswered. Early in the morning, something told me to go and pray for him. He always told me "trust your instincts; your gut'll tell ya," and I always listened, so I stopped the car he fancied (in the name of religion, which he didn't) in front of the Mission Church on Tremont Street. I climbed the stone steps and made my way toward the altar in pre-dawn shadows beneath the statues. I wrote "Joe Rein" on a petition, folded it, and put it in the basket nearby. I whispered the Memorare and lit a candle.

They told me Joe died later that morning.

I cried.

After this essay is published on *The Sweet Science*, I'll half-expect the phone to ring, like it always has. But there will be only silence—an unfamiliar, aching silence. My plan is to rent a John Garfield movie, old-school cool, and reminisce.

I won't let him die. None of us should.

November 12, 2013

Wonderland

When the bell rang to begin the tenth round on June 7 at Madison Square Garden, Miguel Cotto headed out from his corner to meet the middleweight king, who never met him. Sergio Martinez, battered and bloodied, was fighting his corner instead. "Uno mas," he pleaded. "One more." But he was not adamant. His chief second was. "No! It's my responsibility!" he said, and stopped the fight.

Cotto watched from a few yards away, his pulse slowing; his face a detachable mask. He had made laughing stocks of those pundits who one year ago couldn't imagine he'd challenge middleweights, never mind topple a king. But Cotto isn't the gloating type. His stoic presentation covers a heart three sizes too big, and he began his reign with kind words and a kiss for Martinez.

When Bob Fitzsimmons's freckled fists beat the flesh though not the spirit of the acclaimed middleweight king in 1891, Jack "The Nonpareil" Dempsey's corner did what Martinez's corner did and threw in the sponge. Fitzsimmons, like Cotto, was dominant from the start. He too scored a litany of knockdowns, emerged unscathed, and began his reign crouching down beside the vanquished to "whisper kind words of encouragement into his ear."

Fitzsimmons-Dempsey. Cotto-Martinez. Two fights, one story. Declining middleweight kings deposed by weight-jumping challengers who elevated the humanity of their opponents, themselves, and the sport. It's the Janus faces we expect to see with every fight, the contradiction that isn't contradictory: Darwin during ('Get him before he gets you"), John Bradford after ("There but for the grace of God go I").

Miguel Cotto is, by my reckoning, the forty-ninth middleweight king to enter a long and turbulent succession stretching back at least to Fitzsimmons himself. Between them are names that bring the boxing historian to bended knee: *Hopkins. Hagler. Monzon. Giardello. Robinson. LaMotta. Zale. Walker. Greb. Ketchel.* The twentieth century crammed it full of continental Americans, where the average dimensions of males are middleweight before training camp. Size matters. It isn't a division that easily accommodates the peoples south of the border, and it's no surprise that so few of them have conquered the division. Cotto has emerged as the first Boricua in history to do so. When he appeared at the post-fight press conference, the color of his shirt was purple. Like royalty.

And yet it all drifted past press row like a summer breeze.

If the sweet science were as rational outside of the ring as it is inside of it, King Cotto would have been trumpeted from Anguilla to New Zealand. But the sweet science doesn't make sense. Nearly everyone is confused and many are content to remain confused. And out of this confusion came a perky phrase repeated ad nauseam in word and in print —"Cotto," it said, "is the first boxer from Puerto Rico to win world titles in four weight classes." Variations of this phrase were sprinkled like fairy dust while the true significance of what Cotto accomplished was lost. Lost like Alice in Wonderland. Lost like Malcolm Gordon in NYC. And fistiana's fourth estate, which no longer has the inclination to take a good hard look at what passes off as accomplishments these days, is to blame.

> *But I don't want to go among mad people," said Alice.*
>
> *Oh, you can't help that," said the Cat. "We're all mad here. I'm mad. You're mad."*
>
> *How do you know I'm mad?" said Alice.*
>
> *You must be," said the Cat, "or you wouldn't have come here."*

Cotto won bouts that are counted as championships only in the make-believe world of modern boxing. The facts (said Lewis Carroll better than I) stand in front of us with "arms folded, frowning like a thunderstorm." The facts say Cotto took a vacant light welterweight title by defeating Kelson Pinto in 2004. The most authoritative ratings body at the time was THE RING, and THE RING rated Cotto eighth at the time. Pinto was not even rated. In 2006, Cotto took a vacant welterweight title by defeating Carlos Quintana. Quintana was rated ninth while Cotto himself was not rated in the division because he had never fought in the division —he was handed a belt because he's Cotto; much like the mayor is handed a stuffed animal at a carnival because he's the mayor. Four years after that, Cotto took another dubious title by defeating jr. middleweight Yuri Foreman. That belt traces back to 2002 when one unrated fighter beat another unrated fighter in what was imaginatively called a world championship.

If Cotto is a four-time world champion, then I'm the Cheshire Cat. But it isn't Cotto's fault. He was handed a few belts and for all he knew, he was Henry Armstrong. It's our fault.

> *"Curiouser and curiouser!" said Alice.*

Amateur star Vasyl Lomachenko has been given a hero's welcome to Wonderland. Rightfully hyped for his superb athleticism and skills, he is wrongfully hyped for winning "a world championship" not two weeks ago. Neither he nor his opponent was ranked in the top ten by the *Transnational Boxing Rankings Board,* and neither has anything resembling a claim on anything resembling a championship no matter what they did on June 21. "If it was so, it might be," said Lewis Carroll better than me, "and if it were so, it would be; but as it isn't, it ain't." Then again, we're in the land of make-believe, where facts are flakes of dandruff brushed off Versace suits.

Lomachenko did not earn but was granted an international title shot in what was promoted as his first professional fight and a world title shot in his second professional fight. Grinning from ear to ear is an inconvenient detail that we are invited to ignore; it says Lomachenko was paid for six five-round bouts before his Vegas debut and was thus and therefore a professional with a 6-0 record before either of those title fights.

Promoter Bob Arum told the Boxing Channel that the fast track was all "part of the deal" in signing Lomachenko. Isn't that a peach? Lomachenko wanted to become a champion immediately, Arum wanted to sign him, so Arum made it happen. The only check on their ambitions was Orlando Salido, a dead-eyed spoiler who stymied Lomachenko's first attempt at a title. To get him right back on track, they clicked their heels and there appeared Gary Russell Jr., a bright-eyed tenderfoot absurdly rated number one by Arum's glad-handing friends in the belt business.

Lomachenko's victory over Russell was followed by another perky phrase repeated ad nauseam in word and in print. Lomachenko, it said, "tied the record for fewest fights to a world title." This was, in turn, puffed up by a minute-and-a-half of research that uncovered long-retired Saensak Muanysurin, who won a title in his third professional fight in 1975. Another two minutes' research would have uncovered the sorry origin of that sorry title: Muanysurin won it from Perico Fernandez who fought Lion Furuyama for it though neither were rated in the top ten by THE RING. Not a one of them ever conquered the division. Neither has Lomachenko. Nohow! They brandish decorations and are solemnly declared "champions" by mad parties that profit from the term, while we the press fret about deadlines and smile at it all like white rabbits.

> *"I don't think —"*
>
> *"Then you shouldn't talk," said the Hatter.*

We had good reason to smile Saturday night before the main event when HBO cameras zeroed in on a sixty-nine-year-old man shadow boxing from his seat. It was Ron "The Bluffs Butcher" Stander, who long ago tried to knock Joe Frazier's head off in a bid for the one and only heavyweight throne. I was smiling too, until the commentators had to go and make something that isn't something that is. "After an absence of forty-two years," they said without a great deal of thought, "championship boxing returns to Omaha, Nebraska." No it didn't. Terence Crawford isn't the lightweight champion —not yet. That there's a reality check; it doesn't diminish the fact that he conjured up a young Ezzard Charles in a Fight of the Year candidate to overcome a nerve-racking challenge in Yuriorkis Gamboa. (By the bye, Gamboa was touted as "an Olympic gold medalist, a dominant amateur, an undefeated professional, with belts in multiple weight classes." Can you guess which accolade was first declared by dodos?)

"So far, I don't know what it means to be the champion," Lomachenko said in a moment of accidental clarity. It should be said in chorus with sixty-eight other so-called champions in a sport that has become as fatuous as Lewis Carroll's Caucus-race.

It need not be. If we'd only poke our heads out of the rabbit hole, we'd realize the madness afoot and at least examine our role in it.

After all, even children know that not everyone can win, and that if too many do, it diminishes the prize and the point. Children know that good sense trumps nonsense even when nonsense is common, and that dodos shouldn't speak.

> *They all crowded round, panting, and asking "But who has won?"*
>
> *This question the Dodo could not answer without a great deal of thought, and it stood for a long time with one finger pressed upon its forehead (the position in which you usually see Shakespeare, in the pictures of him), while the rest waited in silence.*
>
> *At last the Dodo said "Everybody has won, and all must have prizes."*

June 30, 2014

Preliminaries to the Big Bout (1916) by George Bellows

THE RINGSIDE BELLE

The Ringside Belle

Mae West Weakens Legs

Mae West burst onto the Hollywood screen like it was hers the whole time. She was fashionably late —*Night After Night* (1932) was half over when she appeared outside a speakeasy surrounded by leering men. Audiences heard her before they saw her; they heard Brooklyn, with a purring lilt all her own: "Aww why don't you boys be good and go home to ya wives."

Behind her a peek hole opened, then a voice. "Who is it?"

"It's the fairy godmother ya mug!"

West received fourth billing for her film debut but was happy to work alongside George Raft, an old Gotham beau. Raft, an ex-fighter with underworld ties, starred as an ex-fighter with underworld ties. It was he who insisted that she join the cast. "Mae," he said, "stole everything but the cameras."

The moment she walked into the club, the white-bread background music switched to raunchy jazz —the music of Harlem. And she didn't walk in so much as bump-and-grind past the doorman for the benefit of him and the rest of what was, but had yet to be recognized as, the weaker sex. "Don't let those guys in," she said with a toss of her head. "They'll wreck the joint."

West wrote her own lines and they sizzled like a New York sirloin. Sometimes they sizzled like forbidden love. Spotting someone in the distance, she put the brakes on her strut and a hand on her hip. "Hey ga-rilla!" she called out. "C'mere—"

Foreplay

Mae West sprang from the loins of a cigar-chomping, bare-knuckle brawler from Brooklyn called "Battlin' Jack." In her auto-biography, she described her father as something of a free spirit with a penchant for "banging physical action" (not unlike how many described her). "My earliest memory," she told a reporter, "was of dad coming home from making a couple of bucks —with a battered physog— and of mother flying around the kitchen with towels, hot water, and funny-smelling lotions."

Battlin' Jack taught her how to box and before he knew it his daughter had, pardon me, fully developed. When asked whether his being a prizefighter influenced her career, she said, "Yes. It made me. You see, dad was always shadow boxing in front of the mirror at home. He wanted to be a crowd pleaser. Well, I got to using that mirror myself... I wanted to be a crowd pleaser too."

When his prizefighting days were behind him, Battlin' Jack drifted into other rackets. Biographers usually say he became a private detective, but it would be more apt to call him what he was —a leg-breaker in the New York underworld. West recalled his reputation for cruelty and how frequently those he confronted ended up in the hospital. "All his fighting was done doing other people's fighting for them," she hinted. At once attracted to and repelled by violence, her taste in men never went far from the familiar. Her second boyfriend was a young boxer with the same penchant for solving social disputes with a punch on the sniffer as her father. When a rival made a pass at her during a date, a gang fight ensued, and Battlin' Jack appeared, escorted her out of harm's way, and dove into the melee. "I watched it from a porch," she said, "politely —not cheering."

She was still close to the action after she became a Hollywood star. On Friday nights, she was found ringside at Olympic Stadium; sitting politely, not cheering. She was at Madison Square Garden when a teenage Sugar Ray Robinson won the Golden Gloves just before turning professional. She saw Henry Armstrong fighting as an amateur bantamweight in San Francisco. He saw her too. "She was there with her manager in all that beautiful white like she used to wear, stunning as ever," he recalled. "She was sitting right in my corner."

Gossip columnists said she was close enough to the action to touch it, and often did.

Her bedroom eyes were looking for "a guy with a nice build," one of those guys said. "He didn't have to be too handsome. And this is something very few people know —what excited her was a fellow with a busted nose or a cauliflower ear. She liked to fondle it, nuzzle it, kiss it."

Mae West has been linked with more fighters than Al Haymon.

"Gentleman Jim" Corbett once left his overcoat and derby hat in her dressing room. She gave Jack Dempsey a lesson or two in the fine art of embracing like you mean it. When she quipped "C'm up an' see me sometime" in 1933, a Hall of Fame ensemble thought she was talking to them. Jack Johnson came up to see her, she said, "several times." Max Baer was reportedly invited to her bedroom and, well, afterward, went to the window and waved. He admitted that it was a signal to a friend that he had won their bet. West laughed. The parade continued. Jim Braddock took one look and moved faster than he ever did in the ring. (She recalled a conversation with him about, pardon me, "uppercuts and grips.") In his autobiography, Joe Louis told a curious story about "a real good-looking white woman with blonde hair" who bought him a brand new Buick he was admiring in a showroom in Detroit and who would buy him one every Christmas between 1935 and 1940. The generous "lady" was never named, though he let on that she was a movie star with whom he had several one-night stands.

With neither altars nor apple-eyed apron-clingers slowing her momentum, success came early and through unexpected channels. A child prodigy, ragtime singer, and queen of vaudeville, she was playing the Chicago circuit in 1917 when the first waves of African-American migrants arrived up from the South. They brought jazz and the blues with them and West became a fan enthralled. It was at a café in the South Side that she first saw the shimmy-shawob-ble. "They got out to the dance floor, and stood in one spot with hardly any movement of the feet," she recalled, "and just shook their shoulders, torsos, breasts and pelvises." West introduced the risqué dance to white audiences and had her first swig of infamy.

Much of what she saw and experienced found its way into the plays and novels she wrote. Her first play was called "SEX." It went to stage in April 1926. She went to jail over it in April 1927, serving ten days at Roosevelt Island for obscenity (minus one or two days for good behavior) and charming the warden into letting her wear silk panties instead of state-rationed burlap. She didn't learn her lesson. In 1930, she published a steamy novel called *Babe Gordon* that flaunted her preference for prizefighters and taboo topics such as black/white love affairs and nymphomania. "Babe was the type that thrived on men," West wrote like one who knows. "She needed them. She enjoyed them and she had to have them."

In the early 1930s, she and her black chauffeur were spied climbing out of a limousine and walking arm-in-arm across Central Avenue in Los Angeles. They went to an after-hours joint near the Dunbar Hotel where they were tied up in a knot at a table. A gumshoe took notes. Around the same time pulp writer Raymond Chandler was writing "Nevada Gas," which featured a rich and "sex-hungry looker" who got a new chauffeur every three months. Chandler was then living on Hartzell Street, a half hour from West's Ravenswood apartment on Rossmore Avenue.

The Hollywood social scene knew the score but kept it on the hush; after all, they had their secrets. West had more than most.

"Is That a Pistol in Your Pocket?"

Rubbing shoulders and who knows what else with West at ringside was a rogues' gallery of gangsters, many of whom branched out from Brooklyn like she did or left on the lam. There was Mickey Cohen in Los Angeles, Al Capone in Chicago, and Owney Madden. She was closest to Madden, a gangland murderer and bootlegger who became the underworld king of New York in the late 1920s. He was chief proprietor of the Cotton Club in Harlem and had interests in boxing —and Mae West. He bankrolled her career and was, for a time, her lover.

She wasn't shy about asking for favors. When she heard that a Joe Louis-Maxie Rosenbloom bout was being negotiated for the Hollywood Legion in 1937, she called Madden and persuaded him to get Louis a title shot instead. That June, Louis knocked the crown off the head of Jim Braddock and became the first black heavyweight king since Jack Johnson. West was there, ringside.

She said that the guys who talked out of the sides of their mouths were perfect gentlemen, but learned the hard way that they weren't exactly pals. Three of them, one an ex-member of the Capone gang who used to work for her, held her up while she sat in her limousine in 1933. "Throw out your poke and let's have the rocks," she was told, and off into the night went $17,000 in diamonds and cash. She testified at the trial, despite receiving phone calls of the "or else" type. She knew where to turn for protection. Prospective chauffeurs were asked about their ability to bust heads, not brake safely. A procession of professional boxers was hired, among them a future world champion named Albert "Chalky" Wright.

Chalky was a frustrated featherweight who needed a weekly paycheck to keep what little he had. West reportedly did better than that: she handed him the down payment for a house he wanted to buy for his mother and paid for his divorce. He would drive her to the fights at the Olympic Auditorium on Tuesday and Friday nights in a chocolate-colored Rolls Royce; she would slip him a C-note and away he went.

Chalky, no stranger to vice, preferred bourbon to horses and horses to home life. If the word of a private investigator is to be believed, he preferred Miss West to everything else. "I am not the chauffeur," Chalky supposedly told an acquaintance when asked why he didn't always wear a uniform, "—I am The Man." Moreover, he admitted he was in love with her.

She loved him right back. When she heard that his boxing career had stalled out because of mismanagement, she sponsored his comeback and applied pressure behind the scenes to get him a title shot. She even hired his brother to take his place as her driver, to "keep it in the family." When Lee Wright, a welterweight, got himself arrested for shooting light heavyweight Cannonball Green while Green was in a phone booth on Sunset Boulevard, she pulled strings and he walked. After all, said an eye-rolling reporter, it was "an accident."

It wasn't the last time she helped a fighter beat the rap. Filipino bantamweight Speedy Dado followed the Wrights into West's front seat and was arrested for waving a gun at three motorists in a traffic incident. The hot-headed Dado might have been better off cooling his heels in the clink because he was losing more fights than he won. Perhaps (pardon me) his legs were weak.

In the early 1950s, Chalky was retired and greasing pans in a bakery for a living. Mae West was, well, back on top in Vegas with a bevy of beefcakes on stage at the Sahara. In 1955, her private life was thrust into public view. Investigators for what she called an "under-the-rock" magazine were making the rounds at boxing arenas in California where, they said, "the name Mae West is as well-known as Spalding." Chalky Wright's name kept coming up. They tracked him to a bar. Chalky, thinking they were producers interested in making a movie about West, took $200 to talk about his months in her employment. "Mae West's Open-Door Policy" appeared in the November 1955 edition of *Confidential Magazine.* It became part of a lawsuit filed by Hollywood against the magazine, though there wasn't much more than a tickle or two among mundane facts about West's cleanliness and generosity.

Her lawyer drew up an affidavit denying any hanky-panky and the ex-featherweight champ signed it, or so the lawyer said. In 1957, Chalky was also subpoenaed to court, but he never showed up. He died thirteen days before the court date.

It was an odd death. Recently separated from his second wife, he had moved in with his mother on South Main Street in Los Angeles. On August 12, she returned home from shopping and heard water running in the bathroom. She called Chalky's name and when he didn't answer she unlocked the door to find his body slumped in the bathtub. His head was under the water and the tap was running. At first, police suspected foul play. A towel rack had been torn from the wall, which suggested a struggle, and they thought they saw a contusion on Chalky's head.

Whatever the cause, the case against *Confidential Magazine* went forward and Chalky's ex-wife's subpoena was in the mail practically before the mourners had left Lincoln Memorial Park. It was still on her kitchen table when the phone rang. "You'd better clam up," she was warned, "if you know what's good for you." She made it clear to the Baltimore *Afro-American* that the caller did not represent the magazine. She said "[t]hose people have too much money and too much power" but would not say who "those people" were and that invites speculation that West's underworld friends were behind it. On the other hand, another witness was told to slant testimony in favor of the magazine, and a third, scheduled to testify against the magazine, died from a drug overdose that was no less suspicious than Chalky's death.

Chalky was no stranger to vice. Word on the street was that gangster Frankie Carbo owned him during the latter days of his career, and no one doubted that he had a story to tell. It turns out that he told it, three years before his death, to a young black pulp writer by the name of Jay Thomas Caldwell. *Me an' You* was published by Lion Books in 1954 and was dedicated to "Chalky, the gentle Hedonist." Names were changed to protect the not-so innocent: "Turkey Jones," the main character, is Chalky. "One Gun Laws" is "One Shot" Wirt Ross, Chalky's manager early in his career, and "Al Smith" is Eddie Mead, his last manager.

The story unfolds like a deathbed confession. Laws/Wirt, said the Chalky Wright character, routinely "invented fiction for the newspapers," including one that said the fighter was born in México. Chalky had a good laugh at that one: "Ain't that a pip?" his character says. There are more serious revelations that, if true, cast a shadow on his career. For example, the record tells us Eddie Shea knocked out Chalky Wright in the first round in 1933. In the book, a fight manager (who happens to share a first name with notorious West Coast gangster Mickey Cohen) meets Turkey Jones at the Main Street Gym in Los Angeles and hands him $300 to take a dive against "Bobby Shay" in the first round. "That bum didn't knock me out," Chalky's character says afterward. "I dumped." It wasn't the only time he did.

The character of "Tommy White," a short, God-fearing whirlwind from St. Louis who became a double champion, is Henry Armstrong. Chalky's character is offered a fight against the Armstrong character to set up the book's most startling mea culpa. It's found in a scene on page fifty-five:

"Only one thing," his manager told him. "We gotta do a little business."

"Whatever's best," the fighter replied.

"Okay. They want a good guy, somebody with a reputation and you're the only one who fills the bill. But they know they can't take any chances with you. You might beat him."

The record tells us Chalky Wright was knocked out by Henry Armstrong in three rounds in 1938. It is no longer certain that he was. Armstrong's manager, Eddie Mead, is fingered in the book as the man behind the fix. Three pages later we read that the manager was satisfied enough with the performance to invite the main character to New York. It's a matter of record that Eddie Mead became Chalky's manager after Armstrong-Wright and that Wright's next fight was his first at Madison Square Garden, where the spotlight was brighter and the purses were bigger.

It's also a matter of record that Mead was in bed with gangsters on both coasts. One afternoon in 1942, he dropped dead in front of the Park Central Hotel. According to Mickey Cohen, Mead was fencing diamonds back east for him and they were stashed in his coat. Cohen couldn't believe it. He died "with all the f*ckin' stuff on him!" (The police report left that out.) "Boxing and the racket world were almost one and the same," opined Cohen as if we didn't know. "Most boxers were owned by racket people and at one time, six of the boxing titles belonged to guys in the so-called racket world."

Chalky's affinity for white women is also dramatized in the pages of *Me an' You*, including his marriages to two of them, but it stops there. His affair with Mae West is conspicuously absent. There is only a hint, at once suggestive and poignant, that appears near the end of the book as the main character walks toward the ring at Yankee Stadium: *"He smelled a woman's perfume from among ringsiders. It was a white woman's perfume and no matter what he ever did he would never know what to do about it."*

In the end, Chalky's death mirrored his affair with West. Despite the controversy swirling around it, his death was as natural as his love. His autopsy report, dated September 3, 1957 ends the mystery. The Los Angeles County Coroner examined the body and found nothing that would make a mob hit likely. "No evidences of bony injury, either old or recent are demonstrated," it reads. "The scalp is free of any evidences of injury." Nor was he drowned. Tests conducted on his lungs, liver, and heart could not support that diagnosis. The coroner's conclusion was as anticlimactic as a marriage: "aortic stenosis due to old rheumatic valvulitis, inactive." It was heart failure that did Chalky in.

Mae West was present at his funeral.

According to at least one family member, she paid for it as well.

Jungle Fever

In 1927, William "Gorilla" Jones, twenty, was invited to fight in Akron, Ohio by promoter Suey Welch. Jones accepted the offer, toyed with his more experienced opponent, collected his purse, and then went and blew every dime in a dice game. He approached Welch, hat in hand, and asked for an advance on his next purse. He took that and the fever took him. Off he went looking for "dem bones," expecting to double back and square up early. Needless to say, he doubled back with his hat in his hand again. It became a routine until Welch let the dice fly himself and signed him. Jones became as much an indentured servant as a fighter under the new banner. During daylight hours, he was at the Welch Athletic Club on South Main Street; by night he was whooping it up in the red-light district. Welch's father, Akron's police chief, lent a hand and put out an APB to the gambling dens in the city—"Don't let Gorilla Jones through the door!"

Jones spent a few years fighting in and around Ohio. He was a defensive specialist who often loafed his way to a decision win but was more than able to send the crowd home early. It depended on the other guy's ambitions; if those ambitions were too aggressive, Jones would knock him silly. It also depended on Jones's social calendar; if Jones happened to have an engagement to attend, he would plant his feet, so to speak, to get to the dance on time. Late one night before a fight, Welch heard unfamiliar snoring coming from Jones's room and opened the door to find a double in Jones's bed. Jones was you-know-where doing you-know-what.

Late in 1928, Mae West accompanied Owney Madden to the fights at Madison Square Garden. Jones was on the undercard and doing all right. Later, the fighter spotted the movie star and her well-tailored escort in a bar and sent over a round of drinks. West liked his moxie and invited him to see her at the theater. After the show, West found that she liked his heroic musculature too and invited him to her dressing room.

Maybe the walls caved in. Whatever happened, it must have been stupendous because West began bankrolling Jones's career and his luck turned for keeps. He filed taxes on his 1929 earnings totaling $85,000 (that'd be $1,158,430 in 2014), drove a shiny new Lincoln Coupe, sported over ninety suits with sharp cuts and side vents, and developed a taste for diamonds matching that of his new patroness. By the time West was writing her lines for her Hollywood debut in *Night After Night*, the man winked at in one of those lines ("Hey ga-rilla!") was middleweight champion of the world.

It was 1932. Jones made one defense before losing his crown later that year to a Frenchman who looked like something from *The Hills Have Eyes.* He soon followed the woman he affectionately called "The Lady" to Los Angeles. Manager Suey Welch went with him and both were put on salary. By 1934, Welch was supervising fight scenes in a Mae West movie and Jones was earning $750 a week. Welch got out of the fight racket for a while and bought a string of theaters. Jones retired in 1940, and as far as the mainstream press knew, got hired as West's chauffeur, though a chauffeur wasn't often seen walking a diamond-collared lion on a leash along Central Avenue or groping his blonde employer in after-hours joints near the Dunbar Hotel. Central Avenue was part of the black community and the residents there knew what blue-eyed gossip columnists could only guess —Jones and Mae West were lovers.

Sometimes word leaked out. There's a story where some bum made a rude comment about the star and Jones decked him but good. West scolded him for it. "Let 'em talk," she said. "I made four million because people were saying nasty things about me and you shouldn't get in a fight to change that opinion." There's another story where the manager of the Ravenswood wouldn't allow Jones past the lobby to visit West and it was West's turn to fume —she bought the building.

West's generosity to Jones was extended to his mother. Daisy Jones, a retired Memphis school principal, was hired on as a wardrobe assistant and travelling companion and stayed on for eighteen years. She adored West. "She is very kind and I like working for her very much," she told the *New York Age.*

In the 1950s, Jones taught boxing classes at the Boys' Club in Watts until his vision began to fail as a result of adult diabetes. In 1957, his almond eyes were obscured behind horn-rimmed glasses and his total annual income was "zero" according to *Jet* magazine. But West wouldn't let him live any less than comfortably. She had wisely invested much of his ring earnings into a trust fund, purchased property for him, and paid his bills.

He loved her right back. When a motion picture company offered him a quarter-million dollars for his story, he turned them down flat because they tried to make him admit he was one of West's lovers. The Lady always insisted on keeping her private life private and lying to those outside her world was considered loyalty. Jones's loyalty had no price. "All the money in the world would be no good without friends," he said in 1974. "I would never betray a friend who has done everything to keep me on top and let me live the life I wanted to live."

Lowell Darling is a conceptual artist, two-time gubernatorial candidate in California, and president in perpetuity of the Society for the Preservation of Lowell Darling. In the 1970s, he "fell in with hams and muscle heads" at the Cauliflower Alley Club in Hollywood where, he said, old fighters "regrouped en masse to form a constellation of faint stars." Gorilla Jones was among them. He was damn-near blind by then and wore a wig that might have been found at the end of a push broom at dd's Discounts the day after Halloween. Jones's friends at the club knew the truth about the ageless star and the champ, but weren't broadcasting it. "Let's just say," said one of them, "that Mae always had a soft spot in her heart for Gorilla."

Jones was doing all right. He was living rent-free in a small white frame house in Echo Park, the one with the little figurine of a gorilla straddling the lattice fence at the front. His neighbors knew him as a "gentlemanly fellow who would hastily button his shirt if a lady approached the porch where he sat on warm days." Inside the house was a makeshift shrine to his glory years. Darling was one of the few invited inside to see it. One day the phone rang. "That must be The Lady," said Jones as he groped for the receiver.

"Hello Ga-rilla?"

"I have a present I want to give you," Jones told her.

"How much will it cost me, Ga-rilla?"

"I want to give you a telephone for your car so we can talk anytime, twenty-four hours a day."

They spoke to each other, said Darling, "like lovesick kids." Sometimes she sent a car to bring him to the Ravenswood for more than talk. By then, Jones (and millions more) had been in love with the star for over half a century.

In 1980, eighty-six-year-old Mae West suffered a stroke and that purring lilt went silent. When she was brought home from the hospital, she would lie in bed watching her old movies, transfixed by a character as fascinating to her as it is to us.

Early on the morning of November 22, 1980 she went to sleep, peacefully, and took her last breath. I imagine a shimmer of sunlight reaching into her bedroom like a finger to touch her cheek.

The African-American press remembered her as a friend and a heroine. Headlines trumpeted her disregard of contrived color lines. "Mae West: Snow White Sex Queen Who Drifted" read *Jet*. "Mae West Had Her Black Friends" read the *Call and Post*. Columnist Bill Lane wrote that she had "something within that transcended clear skin and sexy hips. She had a humanness that broad-jumped unpretentiously over whiteness and blackness."

Her funeral service in the Hollywood Hills wasn't big and flamboyant like she was when the cameras rolled, like we thought she was. It was an intimate gathering of trusted friends, which is what she cherished most in this world. Gorilla Jones, seventy-four, stood weeping without shame by the casket. Every now and then he'd honk his nose and the wig perched on his head would slip.

West's body was transported back home to Brooklyn to be buried alongside her mother and Battlin' Jack.

Jones was left behind.

He stopped going to boxing shows and the Braille Institute. He stopped going to the store. "After she passed on," said a next-door neighbor, "he just went down." He began passing up rides to the Cauliflower Alley Club; and eventually wouldn't leave the house, wouldn't eat. His once-heroic musculature wasted away to one hundred and two pounds.

On January 4, 1982 they found his body surrounded by his boxing memorabilia, old newspaper clippings, and framed images of The Lady, her bedroom eyes locked on him.

Her bedroom eyes

...*spotting someone in the distance, she puts the brakes on her strut and a hand on her hip— "Hey Ga-rilla!" she calls out. "C'mere!"*

February 12, 2015

Sources and Acknowledgments

Unless otherwise noted, earlier versions of the essays in this book appeared on TheSweetScience.com.

"A Ghost in the Machine": The title is derived from a phrase introduced by Gilbert Ryle in his book *The Concept of Mind* (Copyright ©1949 University of Chicago Press). Census information was derived from "Census of the Slovak People Living in Mahoning County, Ohio," published by the District Assembly of the Slovak League of America, 1922.

"The Boxing Marvel Speaks to Maravilla": Ray Arcel's recollection is from *Corner Men: Great Boxing Trainers* (Copyright ©1991 Ronald K. Fried). Jack Britton's predictions were found in *Providence News,* 8/21/1923; his analysis is in a *Los Angeles Times* series entitled "My 20 Years in the Ring," from March-April 1923. Charley Goldman's quote is from George Plimpton's essay "Ring Around the Writers" (Copyright © 1977 George Plimpton).

"Shazam!": Louis Golding's quotes are from his book, *The World I Knew* (Copyright © 1940 Viking). The post-fight interviews of Sergio Martinez and Paul Williams were conducted by Rodney Hunt for Goossen Tutor Promotions.

"Something to Cheer About": Erik Morales's statements from February 2011 are found in interviews by Elie Sechback and Maxboxing.com's Radio Rahim. "Sport for Art's Sake" was written by Heywood Broun after Georges Carpentier failed in his bid to dethrone Jack Dempsey in 1921. It stands as a source for the essay above as well as an inspiration.

"Bruce Lee in Boxing Trunks": References include "Talking with Leo Fong," by WR on Real Fighting.com; Jerry Beasley's "How Bruce Lee's Jeet Kune Do Techniques Revolutionized Joe Lewis's Karate"; EsNewsReporting's "How Boxing Helped Bruce Lee Become a Legend"; and Bob Birchland's essay "Bruce Lee Training Research: How Boxing Influenced His Jeet Kune Do Techniques.

"Stugots": Paulie Malignaggi's statements about Shawn Porter recorded 1/31/2014 by "Tha' Boxing Voice." Willie Pep's quotes on Saddler I and II found in *Willie Pep Remembers Friday's Heroes* (Copyright © 2008 Robert Sacchi); Pep's interview in *"In This Corner...!": Forty-Two World Champions Tell Their Stories* (Copyright © 1994 Peter Heller).

"A Wrinkle in Time": Resources include Robert Seltzer's article "'Executioner' Visits Prison" (*Philadelphia Inquirer*, 12/3/1992); Archie Moore's "glass mountain" found in his autobiography *Any Boy Can: The Archie Moore Story* (Copyright © 1971 Archie Moore and Leonard B. Pearl); Charley Goldman's recommendation to "finish on your left" was found in A.J. Liebling's *The Sweet Science* (Copyright © 1956 A.J. Liebling).

"The Hyannis Fight Crowd," *"Peu Exposés,"* and "Flim Flam Floyd" are previously unpublished.

"Shane": Nazeem Richardson's statements were derived from "Guard Your Grill Boxing" episode 131. Burt Bacharach and Hal David wrote the lyrics to "The Man Who Shot Liberty Valance," which is reproduced in part in the second paragraph. "The Code of the West" is found in the work of historian Ramon F. Adams, including his book "The Cowman & His Code of Ethics (Copyright © 1969 Ramon F. Adams)." Special thanks to Jack Mosley.

"Onward, Christian Soldier": Freddie Roach's statements were given in an interview with the host of "In Depth," Graham Bensinger. Manny Pacquiao's statements were derived from HBO interviews.

"Reflections in the Red-Light District": Jimmy Cannon called boxing "the red light district of sports"; Floyd Mayweather Jr.'s penalty in the Juan Manuel Marquez fight reported by Dan Rafael of *ESPN.com;* Fritzie Zivic's statements in "You Gotta Fight Dirty," in *True* circa 1959; "Zivic Virtue" coined by Dan Parker; Vinnie Vines fight reported by AP 9/11/1943; Zivic as car salesman in *Pittsburgh Post*, 1957.

"*¡Canelo!*": Saul Alvarez's answer about his ethnicity recorded by MaxBoxing.com's Jason Gonzalez. Special thanks to Carlos Aguirra.

"The Good Fight" appears with permission of THE RING where it appeared in the August 2015 issue. Special thanks to editor-in-chief Michael Rosenthal.

"Where Have You Gone, Harry Greb?": References include *The Fearless Harry Greb: Biography of a Tragic Hero of Boxing* (Copyright © 2009 Bill Paxton), *Tunney: Boxing Brainiest Champ and His Upset of the Great Jack Dempsey* (Copyright © 2006 Jack Cavanaugh), Peter Benson's *Battling Siki: A Tale of Ring Fixes, Race, and Murder in the 1920s* (Copyright © 2006 University of Arkansas Press), and *A Bloody Canvas: The Mike McTigue Story* (Copyright © Andrew Gallimore).

"Somebody Up There": This essay includes information derived from *The Gladiator: The Secret History of Rome's Warrior Slaves* (Copyright © 2000 Alan Baker), "Most Fighters are Scared" by W.C. Heinz (Saturday Evening Post, 6/24/1950), *Sugar Ray* (Copyright © 1970 Sugar Ray Robinson with Dave Anderson), "I Pray With Sugar Ray" by Jovian Lang, O.F.M. as told to John M. Ross (*Milwaukee Sentinel*, 3/23/1958), and "A Portrait of the Fighter Who Did What They Said He Could Never Do" (LIFE, 12/19/1955). Special thanks to Steve Compton, author of *Live Fast, Die Young: The Life and Times of Harry Greb* (Copyright © 2006 S.L. Compton).

"Zimmerman, Boxing, and Civic Duty": See "Gun Violence is a U.S. Public Health Problem" (Celeste Monforton 7/13/2012) for details not otherwise referenced. Dempsey's late-in-life double knockout is found in his autobiography, Dempsey (Copyright © 1977 Jack Dempsey and Barbara Piatelli Dempsey).

"Joe": Special thanks to Kimley Maretzo.

"Wonderland": Special thanks Sergei Yurchenko for his insights regarding early middleweight championship history.

"The Ringside Belle": *Mae West: Goodness Had Nothing to Do With it* (Copyright © 1959 Mae West); *Life* (4/18/1969); Henry Armstrong's interview in *"In This Corner...!"; Mae West: The Lies, the Legend, The Truth* (Copyright © 1984 George Eells and Stanley Musgrove), p. 143; "Snow White Sex Queen Who Drifted" by Robert E. Johnson in *Jet* (7/25/1974); Private detective's statements in *Mae West: Empress of Sex* (Copyright © 1991 Maurice Leonard); *Milton Berle: B.S. I Love You* (Copyright © 1987 Milton Berle); UP (Jack Cuddy, 6/4/1937 and 9/27/1944); INS 12/6/1933, *Los Angeles Herald and Express* (1/16/1934); Jim Murray's opinion in *Los Angeles Times* (4/25/1961); AP 8/21/1957. Details regarding Chalky Wright found in *Baltimore Afro-American* (12/24/1960), *Milwaukee Sentinel* (12/2/1946); UP 8/24/1957, *Los Angeles Sentinel* (8/15/1957), *Baltimore Afro-American* (8/31/1957), and *Los Angeles Times* (August 1957); *Mickey Cohen, in My Own Words: The Autobiography of Michael Mickey Cohen* (Copyright © 1975 Mickey Cohen and John Peer Nugent); Alice Martin, Chalky Wright's second cousin, told this writer that she believed West paid for Chalky's funeral. Archived autopsy report performed by Dr. Gerald K. Ridge, M.D., Deputy Medical Examiner on Albert G. Wright, 8/13/1957 at 1:45pm (rec'd 10/2/2014 from Department of Medical Examiner-Coroner, County of Los Angeles). Details regarding Gorilla Jones found in "Local History: Akron's King of Rings" by Mark J. Price (*Beacon Journal,* 6/8/2009); "Lady Luck's Frown Starts Jones Upward" by Carl Crammer, AP 2/26/1932; *Milwaukee Sentinel,* (11/22/1931); Jet (7/16/1953, 4/3/1958, and 1/28/1982); *Pittsburgh Press* (6/13/1934). Lowell Darling (unpublished manuscript; emails to author); Los Angeles Times, 1/6/1982. Special thanks to Bruce Kielty, Alice Martin, and Lowell Darling.

This book would have been half to none of whatever it is if not for the help of many talented individuals including Harry Otty at Tora Book Publishing, my eagle-eyed editor Deborah Green, the very gracious Lloyd Lelina at Pixelwurx Graphic Design Solutions, and boxing historian/archivist Alister Scott Ottesen. BoxRec.com has my gratitude, as does Dino Da Vinci, Michael Woods, and librarian Diane Parks.

Any talent I have for storytelling finds origins in Georgetowne, a low-income housing project in Boston, Massachusetts. I was one among a misfit crowd who defined themselves in rumbles and the ability to recount them well. The laughter, often through split lips, would split the night in those last years before gunshots did the same. The stories only get better. Some of the best were generated around George L. Combs, most of them true. I recall a summer evening in 1985 when a security guard made the mistake of calling him an intolerable expletive and George, who was sixteen and already reminded everyone of Clubber Lang, lifted him up and chucked him through the air. The number of times he chucked or otherwise injured those who got on his bad side is roughly equivalent to Joe Louis's knockouts and at least as entertaining. George gave me my name. I was twelve and opposed it, but he was resolute and I can't fly, so it stuck. I owe him more than he knows.

INDEX